# When I Lead Why Don't They Follow?

*by*
*Roger Plachy*

**Bonus Books** *Chicago, 1986*

©1986 by Roger Plachy

90   89   88   87   86                                        5   4   3   2   1

Library of Congress Catalog Card Number: 86-81815

International Standard Book Number: 0-933893-21-3

**Bonus Books, Inc.**
160 East Illinois Street
Chicago, Illinois 60611

Cover design: Ruta Daugavietis


Printed in the United States of America

*For Norm, who taught me
humanism.
For Jon, who taught me realism.
For Sandy, my wife, who is in-
variably enthusiastic—and in 1986,
the best manager-leader I have
ever seen.*

# Contents

# Introduction

## How can this book help you?

Some of you have been hired by organizations as *managers* to apply your expertise to technical issues, but you also have to supervise people who work for you. You would like to be their *leader*.

Some of you have been asked to foster a group's interests, but you also have to put together a program and get people to work for it. You want to learn how to *manage*.

Some of you are parents, or public or religious officials, or volunteers who aren't sure whether you should be a *manager* or a *leader,* but you want to be both.

And then, some of you are successful manager-leaders who want to renew your vision of your role.

Manager or leader, you will fail if you do not understand both roles and choose correctly when you should be one and not the other. People who differentiate their management responsibilities from their leadership opportunities accomplish more for their organizations, for their followers, and for themselves, with less personal dissatisfaction for everyone involved.

This book will clarify the distinction between management and leadership, and offer skills you can learn to become more effective as a manager and a leader. You will decide what you are willing to do to improve your performance as a manager-leader. My contribution is to offer you the fundamental concepts that successful leaders and managers understand, and beliefs that will give you a vision of achievement and satisfaction.

Management and leadership preachings are much the same from whatever lectern they are delivered. We are admonished and prescribed to and the theme is always the same: how to deal with other people. But we're being shoved in the wrong direction. The fundamental issue is not with the people we manage; it is with ourselves.

1

The question of your success or failure as a manager or leader rests with you—and with your openness to experience. Who you are after twenty, thirty, forty or more years is something that is not changed easily. You may participate in training sessions and integrate an idea or two into your behavior, but, if you're like most people, over-all change will be nearly imperceptible. The task at hand is to find the courage to change your life. You will be mistaken if you continue to search for techniques which provide leverage over external forces—mainly people—acting upon you.

Growth hurts and independence is lonely. We are used to neither. Maybe we prefer direction because we are unaccustomed to anything else. Perhaps we wake up to discover who we are when it seems too late to do much about it. We need a time just for us when we can determine, in our unique way, who we are and who we want to be, to think and dream, to let fragments of thought flutter by, sometimes stopping and growing in our minds. The beach, the mountains, a rock in the forest, a workbench, a chair in an office, wherever, but such a place for each of us is essential.

What do you want to do with your life? Is what you are doing giving meaning to you? Is it something important to work for? Does it measure up to what Frankl says is our basic motivation of a "will to meaning"? Do you want to be a manager or leader? Or are you allowing yourself to be caught in the bind of trying to perform in a role for which you have no real desire.

Jung speaks of a meaningful, symbolic life; Gandhi, of self realization; Yeats, of completion; Eliot, of a condition of complete simplicity; Montaigne, of living the life that God has given and to be oneself; Tagore, of Dharma—each man's destiny, the real meaning of his self. The essence of man's ultimate seeking is hardly new though we seem to be "discovering" this at each turn of modern awareness. Maybe what the 20th Century will contribute, at least more loudly than other centuries, is the distinct correlation between our desire to live, and longevity. The way we live can be lethal.

# Chapter One

## Management and leadership are not the same thing

Do you think of management and leadership as interchangeable terms?

If you are always trying to be both a manager and a leader to your followers, quit confusing yourself and them. There is a proper and necessary role for a manager, and a separate role for a leader. Don't confuse one for the other.

Let's look at leadership first. A leader expresses values that match ours.

Including anything more in the definition begins to identify the transition of a leader into a manager. Lock into your mind that a person we call our leader is a person who states or accomplishes what we believe—our values. We own the values. This other person happens to believe as we do.

Our relationship with a leader is an emotional tie: that person is talking about ideas that are important to us, trying to accomplish what we want to accomplish, doing something that we admire.

The moment we empower a leader to speak and act for us, he or she becomes our manager-leader. Empowerment is the point of transition from leadership to management. Although we rush to admire a person who takes command courageously and makes decisions decisively, such a person is acting as a manager, and is our leader only if he or she was empowered to act for us.

Let's review the process of how we designate a leader in a group. It can begin when we realize that one person in our midst is expressing our values. As more of us defer more often to this person, the group acknowledges the emerging leader as accurately reflecting its values. We are willing to grant authority to this person to move forward in our behalf and pursue goals that exemplify our values. In short, this is a person we are willing to trust.

Leadership can also occur when someone proposes a goal and we agree to pursue it.

We follow tentatively. We follow even though we may not agree with each decision this leader-now-manager makes. If we find that the manager makes too many decisions inconsistent with our values, we will not follow. The manager is no longer our leader.

Most managers do not start as leaders. They are appointed to represent an organization's values and to accomplish its goals. These managers assemble or inherit followers and ask them to subscribe to the organization's values. An organization will tolerate followers' values different from its own as long as the values are not adverse to the organization. When the followers' and the organization's values are in agreement, the organization manager is also a leader. The manager who rejects the followers' values and demands excessive adherence to the organization's values disqualifies him or herself as a leader, but remains a manager.

If the manager supports the followers' values, he or she will be acknowledged as their leader. When advocating values in conflict with the organization's, a manager leaves the organization emotionally (though remains in name until his or her authority is rescinded).

A manager given authority over followers in an organization should not presume to be their leader. A leader commissioned by a group to speak for its interests should not presume that he or she speaks for the group on all issues, or that the values of the group will not change. A group may have a number of leaders—

at the same time, according to the issue, or over time if the group changes its values.

In sum, a person is our leader only when he or she agrees with our values. We can accept a person as a leader from afar—the person may never know that he or she is our leader. Nothing overt must happen. The leader does not have to be named. On the contrary, when the leader is named, the leader becomes an official representative—a manager.

Should the definition of leadership include the notion of charisma? Don't leaders have some sort of aura about them which majestically draws people to them?

A dictionary defines charisma as a divinely conferred gift or power; that special spiritual power or personal quality that gives an individual influence or authority over large numbers of people; the special virtue of an office, function, position, etc., which confers or is thought to confer on the person holding it an unusual ability for leadership, worthiness of veneration, or the like.

The divine inception requirement probably puts the gift out of reach for most of us. However, it ignores leaders who any creditable Supreme Being would disown, or that some leaders have denied the existence of any being more supreme than themselves. While we have witnessed leaders who have distinguished themselves in their office to the benefit of those who came under their authority, we have also known criminals who have raped and plundered under their banner.

A large number of people need not be involved; leadership can exist between two people.

There is no consistent charismatic effect on the person according to the office held. The office holder must earn the respect and admiration of the people. If they distance themselves from the people, office holders will be thrown out—the manner of departure depending only on the society. Office holders remain in office when they help people achieve popular goals. If respect and admiration are what people really mean when they say charisma, so be it. Sorry, no ground-shaking sensations or romantic sparks, however.

Perhaps we can grant an uplifting spirit within the definition of leadership. When we have vague, incomplete thoughts floating around in our head, we appreciate someone who pulls them together and makes sense for us. We admire people who think clearly to the central issues and convey confidence in their understanding.

We appreciate someone who looks farther into the future than we do. While we're still lost in the details and turmoil, a leader envisions results and states them to us vividly. We feel the rush of energy to pursue worthy goals, especially in imaginative and clever ways. If nothing else, charisma certainly is a nice word to describe these special moments with another person.

The aura of leadership must not be mistaken for an ability to manage. Heros accomplish spectacular feats and are acclaimed. People cheer and gather around. Heros should not assume that if they lead, the people will follow. If the people do not ask the hero to lead, he or she may not. Heros who are asked to lead may not have the ability to manage—they will be discredited as managers if they try. Worse, they may tarnish their leadership image. We should allow heros to bask in glory but only for a moment.

Most people do not aspire to be a leader or a manager. Maybe they have been conditioned to avoid such responsibilities after having observed the tenuous nature of the positions. Secretly, I suspect, people would like to stand in front of the masses, say mystical words, have the people achieve wondrous things, and be venerated. People want history to honor them.

If we are not capable of greatness, we seek a person who is. We realize that someone has to take responsibility to speak for the collective will. Our fondest hope, however, is that the person who aspires to speak for us will not speak for personal ambition. We so dearly want a manager-leader who cares about us.

We have not been able to isolate the chemistry, the special feeling between the manager-leader and the followers. We can't put our finger on it. We watch people stand on their toes to get a glimpse of the person up front. All we know is that the people feel good about the person.

Sometimes we disagree with a manager-leader's values and do not understand why he or she is embraced by the people. How, we ask, can these people be so stupid as to follow such a charlatan? Why do they do what the manager-leader suggests or demands?

Consider the emotional bond between a manager-leader and followers. Followers *feel* good because of the values expressed. Feelings are not tangible, something to be explained easily. Viewed objectively, we cannot know whether the people are following a leader who truly expresses their values or whether they are following a leader who is obtaining compliance. What we cannot ignore is that the people are following.

Maybe our values are better. Perhaps the people will realize that their values are not truly what they thought they were or will discover poor or selfish administration of the office. They may withdraw their favor for the manager-leader.

Why people follow is the difference between leadership and management. When a manager moves forward to achieve an objective, and the people follow because they have to, the manager is only a manager. When the people follow because they want to, the manager is also a leader.

A leader, then, is a person who expresses values that match ours and who appears to have the ability to manage us in the pursuit of goals that exemplify those values.

The definition of a manager, unfortunately, still connotes a person who retains authority, makes decisions without concern for the people involved, and responds only to the organization's requirements. Followers don't like this kind of treatment; they want a manager-leader who will look responsibly at the goals and needs of the organization as well as their goals and needs.

The challenge of managing and leading is to bridge the conflicting goals and needs of the organization and followers. People are motivated differently. Human discord is natural. There is no fundamental truth that will show us once and for all how to manage people, especially when they do not agree with our decisions. Such a search for enlightenment, particularly for charismatic leadership, is an illusion. The optimum moment of organizational effectiveness, when everybody wants to do the same thing, even for different reasons, is better viewed as a coincidence.

Here is the enigma. Management and leadership are distinctly different, yet one cannot exist without the other. Managers who rely on technical knowledge and ignore the human influence on their position fail—by all decent standards. Leaders who rely on their relationship with their followers and ignore the need to plan, organize, and control fail—by all measureable standards. Management without leadership is hollow. Leadership without management is fruitless.

Ironically, most managers and leaders I've met have not studied much about management and leadership—its meaning, process, methods or, most importantly, its nature as a human relationship. Even among the few who have studied, there is a gap between what they know and what they do in a practical sense when they interact with other human beings. The lessons in this book are for people who want to be manager-leaders, and who want to be more effective and action-oriented when they interact with their followers.

Wherever it is practiced, the principles of management and leadership are the same, but the applications differ according to the requirements of each situation. Leaders must learn to learn from one another. I have never met a leader committed to his responsibilities who did not want to do a good job.

Not every one was successful—some because they were not personally capable of developing the necessary talents and knowledge, most because they had jumped into a management or leadership role without understanding its principles and with techniques that were disorganized and unfocused. They did not act from a solid foundation; they did not understand their purpose and role.

Reading these lessons will not ensure instant success as a

manager-leader. Developing your abilities will take time, hard work, and plenty of self-examination. You are your own person; you are unique. You will develop your own style. It should be that way. Perhaps you will think from time to time about your influence on other people, your place in their lives. You are entitled to your own style, but not every style is acceptable.

One of the purposes of these lessons is to ask something of you—a *humanness* in making decisions involving people. The guidance you provide, or fail to provide, will create an environment which will strongly suggest to your followers the amount of effort and earnestness with which *they* should fulfill *their* responsibilities. When it is demanded of them, help them to be fully understanding human beings.

When you and I place our faith in a manager-leader, we do not abdicate our human right. We give a manager-leader a portion of our life, and that is the most any human being can do. Your followers want certain qualities in you, basically what they would ask of any human being. They expect to be treated with dignity and justice. Don't you?

A personal conversation would be the best way we could study management and leadership together. Presenting thoughts in writing has its advantages, but it is weakened by an inherent communications fault: I am not able to test what you understand from my message, and you cannot test your understanding by questioning me.

I don't know you; I don't know what needs have motivated you to read these lessons. Each of us learns best when information relates to our particular stage of development—to our needs. Standardized programs do not meet the precise needs of each participant, and parts of a program may frequently be considered irrelevant. A written program is necessarily a predetermined program, but we will use a method which will help you as much as possible despite this limitation.

First of all you have to relax. You need time to stop and consider the concepts and techniques of management and leadership. You can't be forced, and you can't be rushed. You must want to learn, but that is entirely up to you. The burden is squarely on your shoulders to make the lesson relevant for yourself.

Stop for a minute. Put down the book and ask yourself: Why am I reading this? What do I intend to learn from it? Write your answers, and don't continue reading until you have a list. It will take you more than just a few minutes to consider these questions carefully.

Here's our problem right in front of us. Did you stop, as suggested, and write, or at least think about, your reasons for being here? Perhaps your reaction right now is, "Oh for God's sake, I know why I'm here; I don't have to stop and think about it, much less write my reasons on a piece of paper!" Okay, I accept your statement. Now let me explain why I am doing it this way:

You can speed through the physical number of words in this lesson and the ones to follow in relatively short periods of time, but in doing so you will accept or reject quickly what is written on the basis of how the ideas test with your preconceived notions. I am just as concerned with your acceptance as with your rejection. You may accept concepts and techniques with an obvious message, but the subtle implications may be more beneficial.

Think back to a learning experience when you were taught to perform a specific task.

The explanation may have sounded fairly obvious, but the execution probably left something to be desired.

Explanations of what management and leadership are may also sound obvious but the concepts and techniques we examine will require different concentration and practice. We are not talking about a mechanical, perfectable process. We are talking about human nature. If I were with you now I would try to find some way to emphasize this point in order to dramatize the importance of what I am saying. Human beings are complex, and we know so little about them. Learning about human nature means thinking about your preconceived notions, your feelings and emotions, not merely testing new information and accepting or rejecting it.

I resist giving direct answers to groups in a learning experience until I think the question has been adequately considered. Participants frequently become frustrated with me for not answering quickly enough, but it is not so much my answers that they learn as it is the conclusions they derive from considering what they, and I, have discussed.

Here, also, I am concerned with the way you will consider what I am writing. I will ask a question with the expectation that you will stop and take time to develop the subtle implications in an answer. Sometimes your answers may take days to develop. Take the time; it will be worth it. In some cases I will give you answers from my personal discussions with other students so you can compare your thoughts with what others have said. Get a group to search through answers together—make it fun.

This is not an exercise in treating you as a child, as many people feel in some programmed learning exercises. Rather, this has proved to be an effective way to learn for most people in most situations.

It is also a way of giving you my ultimate trust, recognizing and admitting that my word is not law. My word is my opinion. You are entitled to your opinion. While I may disagree with your opinion, I cannot deny it. I accept that you may not change your opinion. Further, I demand that you do not change if you have searched your answer to the depth of its meaning, openly, and are willing to defend it.

Now, what about the question: Why are you reading this?

Let's see what other people have told me about why they took the time to consider management and leadership, and then let me give you some reasons why I think it is important to do so. Other people have joined in discussions to:

- be more effective
- improve
- be able to plan better
- do a better job of establishing priorities
- become a better decision maker

- organize themselves and the job to be done
- understand people
- get along better with people
- help their employees learn to cope with different problems
- do a better job for their supervisors
- stand up to their supervisors when they know they're right
- work more effectively with their peers
- communicate more effectively
- learn about themselves

My first reaction to these reasons is to accept them; they are not arguable. They are what other people have told me about their motivation. Perhaps your reason for being here is in the list. If it is not, it is now.

To be more effective is a very meaningful reason to me. It's a worthy goal. We all want to be effective, and we can all learn something about being more effective.

How we respond to change is at the heart of being effective. We all realize that much change is occurring, and that it is occurring faster and faster—except with people. We are held back because we do not cope well, with others or ourselves. We tend to maintain an image of ourselves and a set of assumptions about others that we learned in our earliest years. We have not earnestly tried to use the knowledge we now have about human nature and human behavior. But it is not too late to begin.

We must begin now. We know so little about people, but we are learning. The momentum is there to improve, to get on with a better life. As a manager-leader you are in a position to keep the momentum going, to help others cope with change more effectively.

## How to be more effective

The following scale designates eight different ways to interact with your followers. As a manager-leader you will have to choose one of them in every situation. The more you choose to manage, the less you choose to lead, and visa versa. We'll start you on your way to be more effective by asking you to be more aware of the choices that you make.

1.  In a diary, keep a record of the times when you chose to manage and the times you chose to lead.

## Manager/leader option scale

Manager

You decided what would be done and announced your decision

You decided what would be done and gave an explanation in order to persuade

You developed what would be done, asked for a reaction, then decided what to do

You developed what would be done, asked for a reaction, then blended what you thought with the reaction you received

You identified a problem, asked people to identify ways to solve the problem, then selected the best option

You identified a problem, asked people to identify ways to solve the problem, then joined them to select the best option

You and the people identified and solved problems together

Leader

After a problem had been identified, you specified limits for possible solutions, and let the people identify ways to solve the problem and select the best option

2.  Were you successful or not so successful with the options that you chose? Might you have been more successful if you had chosen a different option?

# Chapter Two

# What does it mean to manage?

Here's the first step in our learning experience, another place where you should stop, put the lesson down, and search for an answer to the question. You may want to jot the question down on a card and carry it with you for a day or so. You may want to ask some friends what they think, and take some time to talk about answers.

How long do you talk about the question? Until you have an answer. Three hours is not too long to explore attitudes and feelings about the meaning of management, to find a definition which is reasonably acceptable. Some people get "antsy" after one-half hour; others find a new dimension in searching and don't want to quit even after they've been at it six hours.

You will probably start by listing specific duties and general attitudes involved in managing. This is good because it shows the complexity of the process. From this complexity you can begin to understand the real foundation of your role as manager.

What does it mean to manage? Here are some of the things other people have thought were important:

- teach
- know what's going on in your area of responsibility
- staffing
- be available to your followers
- report what's going on to people who need to know

- run the show
- act as a traffic director
- seek improvement
- give confidence to those around you
- be fair and just
- feed information from your supervisors to your followers
- feed information from your followers to your supervisors
- run your department
- control employees
- apply your technical qualifications
- direct the activities of others
- arrange for people to be where they should
- see the relationship among jobs
- coordinate employees, visitors and administration
- upgrade service
- help solve personal problems
- reprimand
- be observant
- develop policies for your own area
- implement policy
- manage services and direct personnel

Add your own thoughts to the list if they aren't there already. Then ponder the impact of all the thoughts. Nothing on the list is wrong. But a common definition of management must help each manager through the differences in individual situations, yet be meaningful in all. It seems terribly clumsy to enumerate so many duties each time we need to convey the meaning of management or focus on why we are managers. As you study the list you will begin to see similarities among the items. Think of yourself as a manager in one area of an organization, and then think of a person who has a similar role in another area. Are the jobs different? Yes. Are they the same? Yes. They are different and yet they are the same. Where can we find some common ground? How can we synthesize our list?

One common denominator is people. All managers have followers. Doing something also sifts out as another element, even though the things done in various situations are different. So we seem to have two elements: people and doing something. One group liked the definition helping people to do things; another group liked utilizing human resources to get the job done. One group finally settled on influencing people to achieve objectives; another group settled on accomplishing objectives through people. I like one of the oldest definitions to be found: getting things done through people.

Remember, we are starting at the beginning, with a foundation from which we can build more meaning. All the specifics of management are really quite meaningless unless we first understand the essential nature from which they emerge. The error usually made in the development of managers is that the foundation is rarely constructed.

There is a meaning to each of the elements in the definition, "getting things done through people." We will explore "through people" later. What does the element "getting things done" mean to you? Stop and think about it.

Getting things done means being positive rather than finding a variety of reasons why something can't be done. It means being achievement oriented. There is no room for excuses; if you don't accomplish your tasks, you have failed. There is no passing the buck. An old friend once said, "Do something, Plachy, even if it's wrong." Well, that may be stretching the point a little, but I knew what he really wanted to tell me.

If one of the followers you manage has a poor attitude with certain kinds of work, it is your fault if nothing is done about it. If supplies run out because one of your followers can't take an accurate inventory, it's your fault if nothing is done about it. If a report isn't completed and filed, it's your fault if nothing is done about it.

If clients do not receive a favorable initial impression of the organization, it's your fault if nothing is done about it. If you are the administrator and some of your department heads are unable to maintain expenditures within budget allocations, it's your fault if nothing is done about it.

Are you beginning to think I'm pointing a blaming finger

at you for all the mistakes that occur in your area of responsibility? I'm reminded of a comment by a former NHL goalie. He asked fans how they'd like to have a job where every time they made a mistake, a big red light went on and 20,000 people jeered. Actually, to make life just a little more miserable in the illustrations mentioned here, I could point out that it was your fault the situation occurred at all. Why didn't you prevent this from happening?

The point is the unfortunate organization life style we might call "blame assessment." The question always starts with "who?" The real questions managers must ask begin with what, how, when, where or why? Getting things done has nothing to do with who is going to get caught; it means that when a manager anticipates or confronts a problem, action is taken.

I think of a large company in which many of the managers were nearing retirement age. Some of them just weren't willing to take risks any longer. Someone had to ask them to step aside to let younger people have a chance at doing something. This absolutely horrified the company, but it had to be done. The younger people were willing to risk and to be measured for it. What would have happened if the primary manager had waited eight or nine years until some of the older managers had voluntarily left the system? The company wouldn't have progressed to its goals, and perhaps may even have regressed. Normal rotation was not the answer. The primary manager had to ask himself: What should I do? Do we lose years? Do I sit on my duff waiting for events to take their own course?

A rough job? Absolutely! But when the situation was faced realistically, paid early retirement was an excellent solution. Notice the word "risk." Doing nothing has an element of risk; being positive to get things done is all risk. I'm talking about an attitude, not a technique—the way you believe, not the way you behave. Doing nothing, that is, standing away from a situation so it can resolve itself, is an appropriate response in some situations. That's not what I'm talking about here.

Managing is a challenge, an opportunity. It's a chance to be meaningful. It is not being "at fault," or being "caught." It's the difference between heads and tails. Management equates with the possibility of achieving, not failing. It's positive, forward thinking, not negative and static. Some people fail as managers because they do not want to accept the responsibility. The old saying still stands: If you don't like the heat, stay out of the kitchen.

Perhaps a dialogue from one of my group discussions with some hospital managers will illustrate my feelings. I was saying: "I'd get very selfish and indignant if I were responsible for patient care but other people were servicing my patients and I had nothing to say about their service. I want to know about it, and I want to have something to say about it, because I'm being held accountable for the care of the patients in my area. If the patients are not being serviced properly but you tell me I can't do anything about the person whose job it is to perform the service, that's inconsistent and incongruous."

She: "It's pretty hard to keep these people out if they want to be there. When the lab wants their specimens, they want them."

Me: "Well, lab or no lab, if their personnel shouldn't be in the area at a particular time I want them to stay out. The important objective is the care a particular patient gets. If it's important for a patient to eat in peace, he should eat in peace and not be interrupted. I realize the lab has scheduling problems, too, and I want to cooperate, but I don't want to be subordinated. I know we're on a team and we have to work together. Similarly, I don't want to be subordinated to the schedules of food service, materials management, the laundry, housekeeping, building and maintenance without having them consider my problems. I believe I ought to have something to say about the way they service my area and my patients. That doesn't mean I have to supervise everybody— have direct responsibility for the housekeeper, the laundry people, the lab personnel—I only want to have something to say about them, and in some cases, to them. Like the admitting department, yes, the admitting department, too. If the patients come up to the unit disturbed at the way they have been introduced to the hospital, I want to have something to say about it.''

She: "To whom?"

Me: "To the admitting office."

She: "The admitting office? Well, that's very nice. But do you realize there is very little you have to do with the way they admit patients, how housekeeping cleans up, when they serve the trays, and you—I mean—okay, I can't even get the soap dispenser fixed. I go direct to the department and after 45 minutes of talking, the head of the housekeeping and head of engineering say, 'Okay, I'll give you the gaskets and you have your people put them in,' and then, you know, you have the labor contract and no way does it say that the people in building management will put in a gasket. So when you get ready to wash your hands it still doesn't work. Now you have already talked to the department heads. You don't have anybody else to go back to except to your supervisor whose hands are equally tied because you already talked to the department head. You can't take every little thing to the director, you know; you'd be in there all day. You'd like to have a lot to say about how they do things. It has been my experience you have very little to say. You just have to wait and walk a tight wire and don't make waves. I'd like to be able to say I am the manager of my area, but I'm not, and I don't know how you can rearrange it. I mean, we can't even say to a housekeeper in building management, 'Today so and so patient is sick so I wish you'd mop here.' You have to call the supervisor and tell him you want the man to mop there. You can call your supervisor but that would just be one more thing to do, call her and tell her to call him and he comes down and tells the man. By that time, it's too late. So it's very nice what you just said, but it doesn't work that way, and I don't know who you're supposed to go to after you go to the different department heads."

Me: "You don't think I sound very realistic."

She: "Depends where you're at, what hospital. Maybe in a smaller hospital you might be able to do that."

Someone else: "No, even in a small hospital we have similar problems although maybe not as big."

Me: "Well, let me say two things about this: First, I didn't say how it was but how I'd like to have it. I'm not going to change attitudes tomorrow but that doesn't stop me, or you, from saying I'd like to see some changes. Second, if you don't, as a head nurse, demand the changes required to give effective patient care, who is going to demand them? The building management department or any other department probably isn't going to stand up and demand rights for the patients. For one thing, these departments are usually so far away from the patients they can almost forget what the institution is all about. It's pretty easy to forget what life is like on a patient unit when you're sitting off somewhere apart from the patient care areas. The only time you see some of the service people is when they're admitted. No wonder they don't fully understand what life is like on the unit, but you do. What I say certainly doesn't match reality. There's no question you don't have the kind of influence some of us wish you had. But that doesn't negate the responsibility for saying this is the way it ought to be. If I can't look to you to do something, for some action in developing better patient care, to whom can I turn? You're it; it's your job."

There's nothing wrong with not being a manager. Many people who claim to be shouldn't be. Unfortunately, our society has wrongfully attempted to measure personal success with one's ability to be identified as a manager. The follower with the best technical qualifications doesn't always make the best manager, and yet this is the basis on which most promotions are made. "The Peter Principle" is a wonderful satire which considers this phenomenon; you ought to take time to read it. To complicate matters, we have tended to act as if technical qualifications improve with the amount of seniority. While it may seem ludicrous to some people to promote a follower to a position of management because he or she has good interpersonal skills, this is exactly what we must begin doing. I am not excluding technical skills, only putting them in better perspective. Usually, the better your technical qualifications, the more successful you'll be as a manager. Technical qualifica-

tions are generally most important at the first level of management; however, a manager first, a technician second.

Our thinking has to change. We simply can't afford to make
more mistakes about the people we trust as managers. Time is
too precious; our lives are too precious. I don't, you don't, want
to waste time with fumbling management incompetence. You and
I must examine ourselves to determine whether or not we want
to be or can be not only managers but also leaders. If not, we should
step aside. Otherwise, let's get on with our learning.

We can look at getting things done through people in one
other way to clarify its meaning. I find four elements involved
in your job as a manager-leader: objectives, policies and procedures, technology and people.

Objectives are what you want to accomplish—task, responsibilities. They organize the environment and are the criteria by
which performance is measured.

Policies and procedures are your methods for accomplishing—either by general plans leaving room for discretion, or by
listing requirements.

Technology is the technical skill and training required in the
environment.

People make decisions and do things. Without followers you
can't be a leader.

An historical overview might be helpful. Modern literature
about management and leadership started around 1900 when sci-
entific management was introduced. How the job could be done
most efficiently was the burning issue, the challenge. Organizational management was typically given to the person who knew
most about the technology, and, as we have seen, this practice
is rather widely continued today. In about 1925, people were discovered. The classical Hawthorne studies, conducted at the Western
Electric Company in Cicero, Ill., were conceived in pursuit of
technological efficiency, but the human relations approach was
born when the untapped potential of the human element was re-
vealed in the results of the studies. We recognized that concen-

trating on technology was not giving us the productivity by which real success would be achieved. We didn't stop thinking about technology when people were "discovered," but we thought we had found a better answer. A disproportionate emphasis grew. Organizational specialists in human relations frequently took over leadership, or at least shared it. It didn't take long, perhaps 30 years, to realize that emphasis on people was not the final answer either, although, as with technology, many management practitioners still believe treating people well and keeping them happy is the key to effectiveness.

Then the *process* of decision-making and implementation became the subject of a flurry of academic excitement. What kinds of policies and procedures we developed, how well they were written and catalogued, policy manuals, job descriptions, job evaluation plans, and forms received attention—possibly more than was necessary. We improved to some degree, continued to suffer from overemphasis, but did not find a panacea. We were, in fact, avoiding the real issues.

Observing successful manager-leaders, we noticed a habit of setting objectives for themselves, focusing very clearly on them, and measuring their performance in relation to the objectives. Some manager-leaders shared the decision with their followers of how to accomplish their objectives, some even shared the setting of objectives. Management by Objectives (MBO) was born. If the technological and human inputs were focused clearly on reasonable objectives, success seemed assured. Unfortunately, this hasn't worked either, because policies and procedures, technology and people have been given diminished attention.

Some manager-leaders are still looking for a magical answer. I'm convinced there is none, and I think more people are beginning to recognize that management and leadership are mostly old-fashioned hard work.

Which of the four elements, objectives, policies and procedures, technology, or people, do you consider the most important? Don't answer hastily; consider the four elements closely.

Other students of management and leadership have answered the question with emphasis on each of the elements:

"You have to know where you're going and how you're going to do it in order to get there."

"Yes, but you have to know how to get there, what skills to apply, what to do."

"Sure you have to know where you're going and what to do to get there, but without people, who's going to do the work?"

These are all forceful and convincing statements which have been strongly debated. I wonder what you decided?

I believe success rests in a balance among the four elements, not an emphasis on any one of them. At a specific moment, of course, any one of the four will clearly be more important than the other three. In an emergency, the objective becomes most important and people come second. In the next instance, a personal problem of a follower—a people need—might take precedence over the work schedule (an objective) or maintaining consistency in the application of policies and procedures. Technology in the operating suite receives the highest attention. However, a manager-leader's job transcends specific moments and is also concerned with the long term. All four elements are equally important, and a proper balancing of emphasis among them is the manager-leader's job.

Still, there is something very fundamental at work here which pervades all the elements:

Objectives are determined and pursued by people.

Policies and procedures do not develop by themselves but are developed and used by people.

Technology is not important in a manual but only important as it is applied by people.

People are people.

I am not suggesting we should conclude that people are *the most important* element in the process. We need a balance of emphasis among the four elements. This, I believe, is the answer at which we have finally arrived in our search for leadership effectiveness.

Nevertheless, the common thread among the elements, the

foundation which gives substance to the process, is people. Organizations are usually compared on the basis of performance, technology, image or financial resources. Rarely are "people resources" compared. Yet people produce these other, more often compared, criteria. People who are more interested in what they are doing, more imaginative, and more effective are what make successful organizations. People make the difference.

## How to be more effective

Things go wrong. Successful manager-leaders do not become angry with others involved in a mistake or failure. They do not place blame.

Successful manager-leaders accept that they are officially accountable for everything that happens within their realm of authority. Duties may be delegated but ultimate accountability cannot. Manager-leaders have a sense of personal responsibility for events. They want to know what they did that may have contributed to a mistake or a failure. They want to know how to do it better next time.

You need to learn not to be overly concerned with how things went wrong. Learn to focus on the results desired and the relationship involved. Time spent placing blame is time wasted and leads to less improvement and more hard feelings.

1. Make sure that you get agreement with others on what they will do for you. Ordering someone to take on a duty is not obtaining agreement. Ask: Is this OK with you? Do you have any other ideas on how we might proceed?
2. Make an agreement precise—who, what, where, when, and how. Offer help. Ask that you be told when an agreement will not be kept.
3. Applaud agreements that have been kept; confront agreements that have been broken. Do not place blame for broken agreements (so easy to say yet so hard to do). Find out where the agreement broke down.

# Chapter Three

## Is there a most successful method of managing and leading?

What are your thoughts about this question?

The question needs time to sink in. You need time to sort out your reasoning, to sort out other people's reasoning, to understand and test.

Here are some answers other people have given:

- Know your follower's jobs.
- Develop cooperation.
- Make sure your followers understand their jobs.
- Establish goals.
- Develop your own capability.
- Control whatever happens.
- Be a good listener.
- Be responsive, take action, do something.
- Let your followers know you are there.
- Don't believe everything you hear, check it out.
- Set a good example.
- Show interest in what you and others are doing.
- Be hard but fair.
- Compliment people when they do a good job.
- Offer rewards.
- Admit your own ignorance.
- Develop a team effort.

Is any one of them an adequate general prescription? Is it always correct? Will it ensure success?

I can find good reasons to appreciate almost every suggestion, because each one contributes to a manager-leader's success or, in its absence, to a manager-leader's failure. Each is helpful, but I don't believe any one of them answers our question about the most successful way.

We have tried to categorize certain techniques as either right or wrong, and we have confused ourselves in doing so. We have sought to discover the techniques that would result in the best performance. The confusion arose because some of the techniques leaders used in one situation were successful, but the same methods used elsewhere were unsuccessful. A technique had to be either right or wrong. The most obvious answer, that a technique could be both *right and wrong,* failed to occur to us. Study after study attempted to find the magical answer which would resolve our concerns.

What is the most successful way to manage and lead? There is no *most* successful way. You will be successful as a manager-leader when you adapt and relate to the specifics of the situation in which you find yourself. What constitute the specifics of the situation? The model I suggest is objectives, policies and procedures, technology and people. These are, for me, the elements of any situation: Where are we going? How are we going to get there? What kind of skills are we using? Who are the people involved?

There is no *one* best way to ensure your success as a manager-leader; there is no *one* set of specific answers you can use to get through every situation. There can be no book of explicit procedures that will tell you what to decide. Procedures so designed are usually ignored because they are inadequate and restrictive and prevent real problem solving. Too much time has been lost "looking up" answers which weren't to be found. A manager-leader needs policy guides but also the flexibility to apply them to specific situations.

Are there no principles which will guide you toward success? There are, and the first one is, don't be rigid in your approach—adapt and relate your techniques to the situation as it presents itself. We all want to be successful, and we face a natural tendency to stick with a winning method.

Not too many years ago, management and leadership were examined according to their styles, such as authoritarian, democratic and *laissez-faire*. A strong case was made for the democratic style. However, as tempting and promising as it looked, democracy simply didn't work all the time. There comes a time when a manager needs to be absolutely authoritarian and it is the right thing to do. Taking a leadership posture and allowing your followers to participate or consult with you in the decision-making process is also tempting, because some of the decisions reached in this way are of the highest caliber, and, besides, you've got everybody in the boat with you on enforcing the group decision. Nevertheless, participative and consultative management can be absolutely the most inefficient style imaginable when you need a decision quickly, when there just isn't time to work out a consensus.

Think about it. From what you understand about the way people accomplish objectives, does it make sense to think any one approach will always be successful? I think not. The objectives, policies and procedures, technology and people requirements of a situation need to be balanced; there can be no emphasis, in the long run, on any one of them. The success of managing-leading is adapting and relating to the situation to get things done through people.

But is there not, you might ask, at least a better than average way? This is a fair and relevant question. Think again what the objectives, policies and procedures, technology and people, and the common thread of people among the elements. If people are the foundation that gives substance to the process, it seems logical to conclude that a people-centered leadership orientation rather than an objective-centered management process would be a *better than average* bet for successful leadership. The lessons in this book offer explanations and examples of adaptive and relative management and leadership, with a special focus on people.

## How to be more effective

1. Tap the best talent. For each of your followers, identify his or her best talent, and how you can tap it.
2. Encourage your followers.

> Let them know what you expect
> Teach them what they need to know
> Give them what they need to do the work
> Let them do it their way when you can
> Praise what's done well
> Listen to them

3. Pay attention to your people. In the next week or so, find a way to tell each of your followers what he or she has done well and how much you appreciate the effort.

# Chapter Four

# A manager-leader's job is to define the common purpose

Organizations are people, not impersonal systems of coordinated and controlled human effort, something lifeless. The essence of organizations is human existence, for without people organizations do not exist. It isn't enough to say that social structures and social systems are made by people; structures and systems *are* interpersonal relationships. We subtly mislead ourselves when we talk of a person's relationship to the organization. Rather, we are dealing with a person's relationship to other people.

It is simplistic to say associations are simply aggregates of individuals, for we find new human characteristics in the association. Knowing a person individually will not always explain his or her behavior when interacting with another person or with a group. People are different when they are in groups.

The principal difference when people associate with one another is their awareness of what other people expect of them. This is a person's role in the association, and it is real, but let's not wander into the impersonality of discussing roles. Roles are fulfilled, or not, by people, and role expectations are created by *other* people, based on *their* values, not the values of an impersonal organization. Organizations don't have values; people do.

Let's consider a question: In your experience of participating in groups, formal or informal, what properties have you noticed resulting from the association of people? Putting the question another way, what do groups do for and to their members? How do people act differently in a group from the way they act as individuals?

You can have some fun with this question. Take a few days and watch people in action.

Here are some thoughts people have expressed to me about their participation with other people in groups. I have put the responses together in a manner which simplifies them for me; use them in whatever way they make sense to you.

- Common purpose and objectives; related activities and interests.
- Communications among members; education of members.
- Cohesion, support for one another.
- Conformity to accepted ways, discipline for those who don't conform; norms, boundaries, standards.
- Custom, culture, ceremony, ritual, attire.
- Formal management and informal leadership; a hierarchy of membership, varying influence of individual members.

Identifying and understanding these properties of association will help you influence your followers or prevent an undesirable influence from developing. For example, a new member of a group needs to understand the common purpose of the group, the reasons for its existence, so he or she can contribute meaningfully to its effectiveness. Being close to a group or even in it but not really understanding it can be very frustrating.

Group members communicate with one another, whether formally, according to some design, or, more often, informally. It can be very complex. Suppose there are five people in your group. You can communicate as a group of five, or in five combinations of four people, ten combinations of three people, or ten combinations of two people, for a total of 26 possible interactions. There's no question that information exchange exists; it's a question of with whom.

There is a pattern to the exchanges, however. People don't communicate with every other group member; they tend to establish patterns with the same people. Once you understand the patterns in the group and tune in to them, you will be more aware of what's being said. You will be able to get a message to a person indirectly by talking to one with whom he or she usually communicates, and who may be more receptive to your idea. Conversely, you can prevent messages from being relayed to a person by not telling them to persons who you know, according to the pattern, will relay them.

All groups eventually have a manager and one or more leaders. During the formative stage, a newly formed group will have to decide how it wants to organize. Managers may be appointed, by a higher authority, or elected, by the membership. Leaders are never formally appointed or elected, but identified by popular acclaim. A group may have a number of leaders depending on the values the group has or wants.

Informal leadership is accorded to a member when he or she exhibits an expertise, whether it be technical, interpersonal relations, problem solving, sewing or politics. The members look to this person for an opinion on matters of his or her expertise. An elected or appointed manager could find him or herself unable to influence group activities without the agreement, usually tacit, of an informal leader.

The most complex aspect of group management and leadership is the determination of who exerts influence, and how much. The appointed and elected managers almost always exert influence and are easily identified, but the informal leaders may exert even more influence, and their identity is not so obvious. However, they can usually be identified after close examination of group activities, and especially the decision-making process. To whom does the group turn, sooner or later, for a decision or for approval? Who is the resident expert? Who makes things happen? Your efforts to influence your group as a manager-leader will be more effective and efficient if you do not exclude the influence of informal leaders.

If the cohesiveness of a group is strong enough, its members may stick together and support one another in unimaginable, tribal ways. Ethnic, nationality, geographic and professional groups stick together. Cohesiveness or support for one another will work when there is a reason for it, when the member perceives a real value in the reason for associating. A manager-leader must always be aware that some members of the group may also be members of another group whose cohesiveness is stronger. Develop substantial reasons for your members to cling together, and you will build a solidarity of group force which will accomplish tasks beyond your expectations.

Cohesion is similar to conformity—group members demanding certain behavior from each other, taking steps, sometimes covertly, to enforce their standards. A pressure exists to do what is expected. This phenomenon can be extraordinarily perplexing and frustrating to a manager-leader. In order to associate with a group, to be considered "in," people will do and say things that as individuals they simply would not consider. Membership can be that attractive. Again, build a reason among your followers for associating with each other, and they will exert an influence on one another to continue to perform in ways that are beneficial to the group. They will discipline each other.

In a search for obvious identity, people in groups develop a culture or set of customs for their membership. The most obvious of these are ceremonies or rituals, *e.g.* coffee breaks, birthday celebrations, initiations, meeting places—visible associations. Participation in customs or ceremonies or wearing the correct "uniform" depends on the attractiveness of group membership to the individual. He or she will consent and conform as long as membership is important to him or her, although, and this is unexplainable, he or she may deny the necessity or importance of the membership. If a member is willing to participate in the customs of the group, the group has importance.

Recognize these signs or customs as important to group members. They may influence members in subtle ways that are absolutely unexplainable on an individual basis. I remember an hospital administrator who understood group customs very well.

He had introduced a transport service and had attempted to develop cohesiveness. Part of his program included bright, attractive uniforms. Most of the members of the group were young black men who at one point showed their solidarity by wearing necklaces of lion's teeth. One day an assistant director of nursing called and complained that she didn't see why these necklaces should be allowed. The administrator said he would consider restricting the necklaces if she would not enforce her rules about nursing school pins.

Stop now and review the significance of association properties. Your success or failure is measured by how well you get things done through people. You will work with people individually and as members of your group. The properties of their association can help you be more effective if you can develop spheres of influence which work indirectly, so that the members influence each other to help achieve your objectives. This is an added dimension of influence, like the principle of leverage or pulleys in physics, where simple additives can produce remarkable power.

Times are changing. People do not associate just to communicate or support one another or conform or participate in customs; they are more inclined today to associate for a common purpose. More important, more real reasons are taking precedence, but these real reasons must be known to and understood by group members.

What are the real reasons your followers should associate with your group? Real reasons exist, but I usually find them unclarified. Some reasons are old and worn out, but we have honored tradition; new reasons have developed, but we are not completely aware of them.

Each leader and group of followers must understand the philosophy and objectives of the group. Each organization should have a written philosophy and objectives in the hands of its members. Each major division in the organization, each section within the division, and so on to the smallest units, should establish objectives which relate to the real reasons for their association. In the long run, objectives are not established exclusively at the so-called top of the association or organization and passed down but are developed from the thoughts of the many groups and individuals that *are* the association.

How do we resolve the conflicting needs of the individual and the organization in which he or she participates? How can the individual maintain his or her unique personality?

An association of people must find an equilibrium, or state of balance, or adjustment among conflicting interests and needs. It is a manager-leader's job to bring the representatives of conflicting needs into collaboration to find that balance. However, people are not complacent. New equilibriums will be required. The people will want to grow. Growth is a maturing process, a developing, a seeking, an ability to deal with change; a revamping, renovation, revitalization and improvement; a search to do things better and do better things. Growth is not an independent objective; it is a way of life. The needs of the association of people who come together for a common purpose, to serve and be served, are there to be considered. It is the manager-leader's job to uncover and understand these needs, and develop objectives accordingly.

## How to be more effective

1. Obtain a copy of your organization's philosophy and current goals. Study and understand them. Discuss them with your followers.
2. What stake does each member of your group have in the organization's goals? How can you help each follower achieve individual success by helping to achieve the organization's goals?
3. Who are the informal leaders in your group? Why are they acclaimed by the other members? What is the best way to communicate with them?

# Chapter Five

# The measure of success
# of a manager-leader

What are manager-leaders held accountable to accomplish?

Start by jotting down your ideas about objectives. Don't be too concerned with a final product at first. Your ideas will jell better when you see all your thoughts together. Take the time to think about the list. Do some research; find out what other associations expect their manager-leaders to accomplish.

Here are some thoughts others have had about objectives:

- teaching
- enforcing and interpreting policies
- motivating employees
- evaluating performance
- preparing reports
- ensuring sufficient supplies are available
- staffing and scheduling
- improvement
- planning patient care
- communicating all pertinent information
- maintaining good working relationships
- disciplining
- human development

I imagine your list will be similar, including some of these objectives, excluding others, adding new ones. This list will help us get started. Our purpose is to consolidate, and to add if we left anything out.

*Teaching* is an objective if you are a manager-leader in a teaching institution. Otherwise, teaching, it seems to me, is a facilitating function, something we do to help us achieve other objectives. We teach followers so they can accomplish their tasks, not simply in order to know a procedure.

*Enforcing and interpreting policies* is part of an objective. Sometimes we will also want to review and change policies, not just enforce and interpret them. Let's broaden our thinking. Like the policies that are internal guides, there are also federal, state and local laws with which we are concerned. Laws and policies are not objectives merely because they are written somewhere and therefore should be enforced, but because they are guides to help us perform more effectively. Without these directions we would wander aimlessly.

*Motivating employees* is not an objective. It is a subject of itself, and we'll take another lesson later on to examine it.

*Evaluating performance* is a measurement of how well objectives are achieved; it cannot at the same time be an objective.

*Preparing reports* does seem to be an end result. Administrative data, state law compliance reports, and others, are objectives toward which we can focus our attention; they have to stand by themselves to provide information or reference. However, further down our list is "communicating all pertinent information." Preparing reports is one form of communicating, along with other oral and nonverbal forms. We do not communicate for the sake of communicating, but because it is essential among human beings if they want to achieve objectives together. The process of communicating demands special attention as one of our objectives.

*Ensuring sufficient supplies are available* is facilitating, because we might ask, supplies for what? Yet it is an independent process. There is an end result in whether or not the supplies are available; it is measurable. Look at the next item, *Staffing and scheduling*. I see a similarity between keeping supplies and people (a scheduled staff) in the right place at the right time, in the right quantity. I would combine the two, and even add something else. Supplies have a rather specific definition, mainly that they are consumable. Let's not overlook equipment. Suppose we consolidate supplies, equipment and people under the common word *resource* and settle on an objective called *Resource scheduling.* I like the word *resource* because it can connote a whole new meaning of value to the supplies and equipment we use and the people who participate.

*Improvement* is obviously important, but I don't see it as being separable, as an end result, as much as I see it as an attitude.

*Planning* is a process. Every objective has to be planned. This inherent process cannot also be an objective.

*Maintaining good staff relations* is a form of communicating. We maintain good working relationships, we communicate, to accomplish our objectives. Let's include "relationships" with the objective of communications.

*Disciplining* is a teaching process we do with our followers so they will be prepared to do the jobs that are asked of them. I don't think of disciplining as a separate objective.

*Human development* is very much like teaching, a facilitating process, something we do to help achieve objectives. Teaching tends to mean the learning of specific skills and abilities, whereas human development connotes a personal growing experience. Performance measurement is not the skills, abilities or growth developed, but the contribution of these talents toward objectives.

Let's summarize what we have as objectives:

- Laws and policies
- Communications
- Resource scheduling (supplies, equipment, people)
- Teaching (in a teaching institution)

What other objectives should be in the list? Budgeting is sometimes mentioned. Actually budgeting is financial planning—allocating money for specific purposes—and is a facilitating process. However, *cost control* is clearly a major concern of manager-leaders and should be added to our list of objectives.

Let's think some more about our Resources—people, supplies and equipment. Not only are we supposed to schedule them at the right place, at the right time, and in the right quantity, but we are also supposed to protect them. Sometimes safety or accident prevention is included in a list of objectives. Correctly, we have an obligation to ensure that our employees are not hurt on the job. Similarly, supplies are not to be damaged, lost or stolen, and equipment should be used properly. Therefore, I'd like to add an objective called *Resource protection* to our list.

So I suggest a final list of general objectives for a manager-leader, objectives which show a new dimension of influence, a broader perspective, as an integrative relationship, with other groups in the association of people, perhaps some responsibilities not considered or accepted by all manager-leaders:

- Quantity of work
- Quality of work
- Resource protection (people, supplies, equipment)
- Resource scheduling (people, supplies, equipment)
- Cost control
- Communications
- Laws and policies

These objectives provide a workable classification into which a myriad of specific duties can be arranged. They are not, however, written in stone; change them to suit your purpose. On the other hand, don't change them too easily. Time after time they have filtered out in many discussions with groups of leaders attempting to identify their objectives. We need to concentrate on the objectives for which we are held accountable.

Looking at the list of objectives, let me ask: Who provides the action to accomplish each objective? I'm not asking who is responsible to ensure that the objective is accomplished. We have agreed that you are. Let's look at the first objective, quantity of work, and place an "x" in the proper column under manager-leader or follower for who provides the action. Who does the work?

*Manager-Leader    Follower*

**Quantity of work**

There certainly are times when you perform your followers work, but we are concerned with you as a manager-leader. Applying the principle that you are not a manager-leader unless you have followers, you are not managing or leading when you are performing the work. This is not a play on words. Management is getting things done through people and at the moment that you are performing the work, you cannot also be managing or leading. You are getting things done, but not through people. When you apply specialized skills beyond the capability of your staff, you are no less a manager or leader to your followers, but at that moment, you are doing the work. You cannot be managing or leading yourself. When you perform some work to teach one of your followers, you are no less a manager-leader. However, your objective is not really the work you are performing, even though it is also being accomplished, but it is the learning experience you are providing for your follower. I would place an "x" under follower to describe whose hands actually perform the work.

*Manager-Leader    Follower*

**Quantity of work**                                         x

In whose hands rests the quality of the work to be performed? If your followers are actually performing the quantity of work, the quality with which the quantity is performed must inherently rest in their hands. Later, you may improve the quality if a poor job was done, but at the moment the work was being performed, the quality was clearly in the hands of your followers. Let's place an "x" in the follower's column.

|                        | Manager-Leader | Follower |
|------------------------|:--------------:|:--------:|
| **Quantity of work**   |                | x        |
| **Quality of work**    |                | x        |

Think about resource protection (people, supplies, equipment). Who would hurt themselves, who would waste supplies, or who might damage equipment? We are thinking about you as a manager-leader who is responsible to accomplish objectives through other people. Your followers are providing the action. I think we'd have to agree to place an "x" in the column of the follower.

|                        | Manager-Leader | Follower |
|------------------------|:--------------:|:--------:|
| **Quantity of work**   |                | x        |
| **Quality of work**    |                | x        |
| **Resource protection**|                | x        |

Resource scheduling is sometimes difficult to understand. You actually develop the schedule of assignments or frequently decide which supplies and equipment should be used. In which column do you place the "x"?

Who provides the action? Are you present or absent in fulfillment of the work schedule? Do you bring supplies and equipment to an area? The point is, we are talking about getting things done through people—and fulfilling a schedule is not the function of a manager-leader, but of a follower. You are responsible for the scheduling, but other people either comply or fail to comply with the schedule. The followers get an "x" in their column.

|                        | Manager-Leader | Follower |
|------------------------|:--------------:|:--------:|
| **Quantity of work**   |                | x        |
| **Quality of work**    |                | x        |
| **Resource protection**|                | x        |
| **Resource scheduling**|                | x        |

Next is the objective of cost control. Who might spend too much money or use too many supplies?

Both you and your followers? In a way, yes. Followers use supplies and equipment and may make some expenditures, but certain expenditures are made by you only—authority is not delegated. However, let's not forget the meaning of management and leadership—getting things done through people. If you are doing something it is not being done through people, and you are not managing or leading. We'll come back to some of the things you do in a moment. Let's give an "x" to your followers for costs which they may or may not incur.

|  | *Manager-Leader* | *Follower* |
|---|---|---|
| **Quanity of work** | | x |
| **Quality of work** | | x |
| **Resource protection** | | x |
| **Resource scheduling** | | x |
| **Cost control** | | x |

What do you think about communications? Who communicates? Does it sound similar to cost control? I would think so. Both you and your followers must communicate. Again, we'll talk about what you communicate in just a moment. For now, we are only concerned with you as a manager or leader. Your follower is the doer and gets the "x".

|  | *Manager-Leader* | *Follower* |
|---|---|---|
| **Quantity of work** | | x |
| **Quality of work** | | x |
| **Resource protection** | | x |
| **Resource scheduling** | | x |
| **Cost control** | | x |
| **Communications** | | x |

Finally, where does compliance rest when we think of the responsibility for laws and policies?

For some laws and policies it is solely your judgment to determine whether or not you comply. You do not delegate the decision and therefore the decision is not a part of the relationship with your followers. Rather, your compliance is a part of the follower relationship you have with the person you follow, and this relationship also accounts for the cost which you incur or avoid, and the communications you are supposed to accomplish. These are the objectives for which your manager-leader is being held accountable. There are other laws and policies with which your followers either comply or do not comply. That they do or do not comply is entirely in their hands at the moment they decide. They receive an "x".

|  | *Manager-Leader* | *Follower* |
|---|---|---|
| **Quantity of work** | | x |
| **Quality of work** | | x |
| **Resource protection** | | x |
| **Resource scheduling** | | x |
| **Cost control** | | x |
| **Communications** | | x |
| **Laws and policies** | | x |

Think about what we have just done. We have examined a list of objectives for which you might be held accountable. Interestingly, your followers provide all of the action to accomplish the objectives for which you are held accountable. How do you react to a relationship with your followers where you are responsible for the objectives but don't provide the action to accomplish them?

Think about it. This is very significant to your success or failure.

The perception of this relationship by a manager-leader is an acid test. Guessing that "my followers are important to me" indicates a total lack of understanding of the relationship. "I have to work more closely with my followers" isn't very perceptive either. "I have to depend on the reaction of my followers" has signs of awareness. "I'm not doing my job if they aren't doing theirs" is closer yet.

There is a psychological contract you must make with yourself if you intend to be a successful manager-leader. There is a separation between you and the work being performed by your followers. Your success or failure depends on your followers. They provide the action, and you have the responsibility. Here is the foundation meaning of management and leadership, the measure of real success: Your success depends on your followers. Your success is getting things done through people, not by yourself.

## How to be more effective

Make sure that each of your followers has a job description—a statement of the desired results to be accomplished.

The way you state expectations in a job description will clarify or cloud your relationship. Most statements only tell what duties are to be performed, for example, for a receptionist:

*Greets customers and visitors and refers them to the appropriate area and schedules appointments in person or by telephone.*

Duties can be performed correctly yet unsuccessfully. A proper job description statement starts with the result desired and adds the duties that must be performed to produce the result. Thus:

*Optimizes customer satisfaction, service personnel time, and use of facilities by scheduling appointments in person or by telephone. Helps customers and visitors by greeting them and referring them to the appropriate area.*

Identify the duties to be performed. Then think of the result that will be accomplished by performing the duties. Write: the *results desired* by *performing duties.*

The focus is clear. All work can be directed toward the desired results. Discuss, clarify, and agree to these expectations at the start of a relationship with your followers, and periodically thereafter.

# Chapter Six

# The unstated requirement is: Be a decision-maker

What does a manager-leader do to accomplish his or her objectives? What is the process involved in managing and leading? What are the functions of management and leadership? Get your notebook. Write your ideas.

The process involves: planning, organizing, implementing and controlling. The words planning and organizing have rarely been changed. Implementing is a word that makes sense to me, although you will also see the word directing used in its place. Evaluating might be substituted for controlling. Arguments can and have been made about why one word and not another should be used. I'm not too concerned about which word you select: the meaning behind the word is more important. However, you might find the words communicating and motivating in a list of leadership functions, and here I take strong exception: Communicating is inherent in all the processes and therefore cannot be separated. Motivating is not a process, not something that you do. We'll discuss these points at length in other lessons.

Planning is the idea portion of a manager-leader's job, the first step, the conceptualization of what we're up against and where we're going. The time for planning is a time of strategy rather than tactics, a time to gather facts, look at alternatives, set priorities, think about resources, forecast and think of desired end results.

This is where the purposes of the association must be clearly understood and kept in mind.

Organizing is the next phase. We know where we are supposed to be going and what measurements and results we will use to evaluate ourselves when we get there; now it's time to get ready to do something, to organize. It's a time to gather the necessary ingredients, a time for tactics, the specifics, the decision to do one thing or another. It's a time to arrange and relate, to delineate relationships and define liaisons, to recruit, select, orient and train followers, to bring everything in logical form so we can begin to operate.

Implementing is putting all our ideas and the resources we have assembled into action. It's down to the bone of getting things done through people, assigning responsibilities, issuing orders, coordinating efforts, interpreting, resolving conflicts, taking action.

Controlling is the last phase. It is looking at what we have done or what we have failed to do, holding up the criteria which were established in the planning phase in order to measure. It is the point of departure for new plans and programs because we were successful, or, if we have failed, the time to re-examine our planning and then reorganize and implement again, to take corrective action.

All elements—planning, organizing, implementing, controlling—are involved in the process. None can be excluded. Their value to you is as a general checklist. You know you must perform all these functions.

The management-leadership process takes on a different emphasis at different hierarchical levels of the association. Perhaps this is made most obvious by simply placing the hierarchy alongside the process:

| | |
|---|---|
| Planning | Top level |
| Organizing | Middle level |
| Implementing | Lower level |
| Controlling | All levels |

While the top-level manager-leaders must perform all four functions to be successful, they will find a substantial amount of their time is spent in planning or at least it should be. The first level will find most of their time used in implementing, although they must also plan, organize and control. It is only a matter of emphasis.

The thread woven throughout the process of leading is the continual requirement for a decision. Manger-leaders are decision makers. They do not predict the future but make a substantial guess at it. They are risk takers. They take chances, but the better ones leave as little as possible to chance. Knowing what happens in the decision-making process won't make you a better decision maker, but it will provide a guide, a checklist, so you will at least stop and consider what you are doing.

The process and technique of decision making has been under specific investigation for many years, and the more we understand human beings and their mental processes the more we understand decision making.

Decision making can be divided generally into the following steps: (1) identify the problem, (2) enumerate the alternative solutions, (3) evaluate the alternatives, (4) select the best alternative, (5) implement this solution, and (6) evaluate the outcome.

Obvious? I think so, and yet how simply we skip through the process or overlook one of the elements! The first steps are the most critical. How many times have you worked through a number of solutions, selected and implemented one—only to find you had solved the wrong problem? Later, when we talk about communications, we may be able to provide some help in more accurate problem identification. The point is that we frequently act on our first perception of a problem, and often our first perception is not the real problem.

Next, we tend to grasp at the obvious. We have a problem, and the first or second alternative solution that pops into our mind tends to lodge there. It is similar to the mistake we make in problem identification, the most obvious is the first answer.

Evaluating alternatives can cause our downfall when we use the wrong set of criteria. Evaluating alternatives is a process of value judgment probabilities. It's an application of criteria and measurements. In its simplest form, judgment is a combination of facts and values. Aside from determining the real facts—that is, the real problem or the real alternatives—the more difficult aspect of judgment is determining values. Values are personal, hard to explain, and cannot be dissected and examined in a suspended state. They are dynamic. What was appropriate yesterday may be inappropriate today. Values involve questions of right and wrong, and these are so often complex. Unless we have stopped to consider our values in a particular situation, we can hardly expect to make effective judgments. If we are asked to judge for someone else, we have to know their values.

Selecting the best alternative is usually fairly easy if you've done good work to identify and evaluate alternatives.

Implementing is the easiest part of decision making, since it only refers to triggering the mechanism. The explosion after the triggering is the part which might hurt.

Most of the decisions we make involve immediate circumstances; thus evaluation is often simply a matter of observation. Evaluation is more difficult in the long term, because we must avoid prejudging a final outcome. The true evaluation is: How well did we solve the real problem? Did our solution create new problems which could have been avoided?

Decisions are required because our environment is always changing. Change, and how we deal with it, has been a topic of intense interest. It has been considered a principle of human reaction that people resist change. This belief can easily be refuted: People accept changes that they agree are for the better. Conversely, changes that people consider disadvantageous will be rejected. The nub of the problem is in the perceptiveness of the people involved. What a manager-leader believes and what his followers believe may be entirely different. The acceptance or rejection of change is a decision. Whether or not a decision is implemented effectively—that is, whether or not it is accepted by the people who are involved—depends on agreement about problem identification, enumeration of alternative solutions, evaluation of alternatives, and selection of the best alternative. If any of these steps is perceived differently, persons will necessarily disagree with the implementation or decision. Some manager-leaders keep their followers informed of the reasons for a change, believing this knowledge will ensure acceptance of the change. However, decision making is a combination of information and values, and people can disagree with either or both.

Management and leadership always involves dealing with change and making decisions. Look at the parallel between the functions of managing and leading and the steps in the process of decision making:

| | |
|---|---|
| Planning | Identify problem |
| | Enumerate alternatives |
| Organizing | Evaluate alternatives |
| | Select the best alternative |
| Implementing | Implement the best alternative |
| Controlling | Evaluate outcome |

Changes have to be made. Someone has to decide. The buck stops with you as manager-leader. It is your job, your responsibility, to make the final judgment. You are not in a popularity contest. You are not a manager-leader in order to win friends. You are a manager-leader to get things done through people. You will make some enemies, and you will have to stand their rejection. You will need courage to be a manager when you are required to be one.

Decisions are very personal to the person who makes them. Yet as close as the decision is to the person, it is only something the person does. The decision is *not* the person. We can disagree with or reject a decision without rejecting the person. Unfortunately, many people generally fail to make this distinction and thus we find many who have been personally hurt, who have felt rejected because other people disagreed with their decisions.

Some people believe good judgment involves the control of emotions, or even their elimination from the decision-making process. They warn against emotions coming between facts and values. But emotions are in the decision-making process all the time. They cannot be eliminated. People have emotions, and their decisions will involve emotions. Decisions do not, however, have to be "emotional" with all the word connotes.

One of the tragedies of mankind is that we have tried to live in a world devoid of feelings and emotions. We admonished ourselves to keep feelings to ourselves. We tried to act mechanically, controlled. The new psychology wants us to recognize our feelings and emotions, to learn to deal with them, not to be afraid of them, to help use them to find a fuller and richer existence, to appreciate them for the spice they add, for the differences they make among people, for the distinction they make from other species.

The manager-leader has often been considered the agent of the organization, without a personality of his or her own. The organization is not as impersonal as we have traditionally considered, however; we need to consider its humanness. We are no longer interested in playing roles assigned to us, in maintaining an impersonal status, in not becoming emotionally involved in our jobs. We *are* human, we *have* emotions, we *are* involved. It isn't a question of whether or not a manager-leader should be a real person; it's a necessity to learn how to be real.

We have restrained our personal relationships and prevented the development of our ability to deal with them. We made many human errors. For example, we easily equated other people's success with how much we liked them. We are discovering a new richness and enthusiasm when we interact realistically with another person. It is human to be close to another person, if we want to be, but closeness can work only when we understand what to expect from it and how to deal with it. Management and leadership require that we learn about this closeness.

Developing courage to deal with change and working through close relationships with other people, bring us—bring you—again to the personal question: Do you want to be a manager-leader? If you do not wish to be a manager-leader I will respect you for your decision. Management and leadership are too important to be practiced by people who don't care for it. In many institutions I find people who are asked, even required, to be manager-leaders, and many of them simply wish they didn't have to be. They find themselves in their positions only because of their technical skills. Some of them know they are not capable of learning and practicing the necessary skills of management or leadership; others know they can learn but recognize that their preparation did not include these skills. I commend this recognition. I wish we would allow them the right of refusal, the right to practice the skills for which they were trained.

There is an obvious danger of oversimplification in looking for a central description of management and leadership which will help you decide whether or not you want to be a manager-leader. We can probably all identify with the positive side of being a manager-leader, the tremendous swell of accomplishment and achievement. The negative aspects will cause the greater concern. If there is a central description, it is pressure. Managing and leading means making decisions, and more decisions. Followers wait for these decisions. As a manager-leader, you can't wait, you have to do something, frequently without the benefit of full information, and usually what you're doing is in the limelight. Everybody's watching and waiting. The need for a decision, the pressure, will always be there.

If you cave in, it will be as if you fell off your surfboard and were engulfed in a wave so big you wondered if you would ever see the sky again. You will have to be resilient, willing to swim as hard and as fast as you can for your surfboard—so you can ride more waves. The people on shore are waiting, and they expect you to be on your surfboard, not in the drink.

Somehow society hasn't learned its lesson. There are too many people treading water. Why can't associations of people understand that the selection of their manager-leaders is a standard of performance, a perception of their values, a declaration of what they prize, an example to everyone? We have already seen the lack of correlation between technical capacity and management or leadership ability. Success in one set of circumstances, will not necessarily indicate success in a new position. Perhaps this seems obvious, yet manager-leaders are often considered qualified only because they have been in a similar position before. Management-leadership is not a profession with universally accepted standards, and I can't see that it ever will be. The process is entirely too personal.

But this scarcely means that we need not be professional in what we do as manager-leaders. We have a body of knowledge; it is growing and becoming more exact. We are willing to exchange our ideas, and to some degree to be measured, but we have a long way to go.

Are you willing to learn? To keep on learning? To learn from others? To be positive? To make decisions? To take action? To achieve?

## How to be more effective

1. Keep a log of your activities. Then go back over your list and identify each activity as a planning, organizing, implementing, or controlling process.
2. Calculate the percent of your time spent in each process. If you feel as though you spend a lot of your time putting out fires and not really accomplishing what you want, you are spending most of your time implementing and controlling. Most

manager-leaders do not spend enough time planning and organizing. As a result, they do not get where they want to go efficiently.

Good manager-leaders make the best use of their time, always looking for ways to improve the return on time invested. They challenge the way they use their time. What am I doing that doesn't have to be done at all? What should I be doing that I am not doing? What am I doing that could be done better, as well, or sufficiently, by someone else? How much does what I do contribute to my objectives? Who can help me?

# Chapter Seven

# A manager-leader must be willing to be influenced

Think of some of the prominent institutions in our society: business, health care, education, government, military, church. What kinds of attitudes do followers hold toward them and their manager-leaders? A lot of revolution and rebellion.

I'm convinced a majority of the members of our society don't like what's happening to them in their institutions. They want a different kind of relationship. Not everyone is searching for a new relationship, but it is evident that there is pressure for change. Manager-leaders in all institutions must stop and consider what is happening. As a manager-leader you must come to grips with what followers are saying. We are at the threshhold of wholly new forms of interaction, of influence between manager-leaders and followers.

What is the usual method which our institutions use to influence the behavior of their members? What are the usual methods in your organization? Here is what members of some organizations have described as the usual methods used to influence their behavior:

- Fear
- Loss of security
- Strict adherence to rules
- Rewards

- Authority
- Coercion

I have also been told that loyalty, willingness, ambition and understanding are also influences on behavior. Sadly, these comments are few and far between. Fear, punishment, coercion—words from the Dark Ages, and yet they are still being used. Small wonder there is revolt, people are breaking away, seeking new relationships. People don't want miserable lives anymore, and certainly life has to be miserable under these kinds of influence.

What is it followers are revolting against? The central issue between manager-leaders and followers boils down to authority. Followers, I am often told, are rebelling against authority. There is a problem with authority, but somebody has to be in charge, somebody has to make decisions. Followers don't refute this. So what are they rebelling against?

Actually, the rebellion is not against authority but against the administration of authority, the way authority is used. It has been used for punishment and coercion, strictness and adherence to rules, regulations and procedures, one person telling many persons precisely what to do. As one follower said: "You want to be able to make little, unimportant mistakes now and then without somebody right there pointing them out when you can see them for yourself." Is it really any wonder that followers in organization after organization have become apathetic, felt alienated, and have not shown the interest or inclination to become involved? What's the sense, if their individuality and intellect are squeezed out of them? We are told we must grow to maturity, but we are not allowed to act maturely.

Followers are pleading to be heard, to be given an opportunity to participate, to influence. Followers are breaking away and are not accepting regimentation. In their turmoil, their questioning of rules, their unionization, followers are saying that they want to become involved. They want to participate, and they are capable of contributing. Followers are recognizing their ability to withhold performance, and they are using it to demonstrate their feelings and their wishes. Followers are telling their manager-leaders in a dramatic way where their authority comes from.

Is this anything new? No! Our society began with the statement, "Governments are instituted among men, deriving their just powers from the consent of the governed." The logic is more obvious than we have usually been able to recognize. Followers do more than give or withhold authority; followers *are* the authority, for without followers, there are no manager-leaders.

If just power rests in the consent of the people, why has it taken us 200 years to realize it? Let's look at tradition.

"You are not acting wisely," his father-in-law said when Moses complained about the burdens of leadership. "You will surely wear yourself out, and not only yourself but also these people with you. The task is too heavy for you; you cannot do it alone. Now listen to me, and I will give you some advice, that God may be with you. Act as the people's representative before God, bringing to him whatever they have to say. Enlighten them in regard to the decisions and regulations, showing them how they are to live and what they are to do. But you should also look among all the people for able and God-fearing men, trustworthy men who hate dishonest gain, and set them as officers over groups of thousands, of hundreds, of fifties, and of tens. Let these men render decisions for the people in all ordinary cases. More important cases they should refer to you, but all the lesser cases they can settle themselves. Thus, your burden will be lightened, since they will bear it with you. If you do this, when God gives you orders you will be able to stand the strain, and all these people will go home satisfied."*

Moses' father-in-law may have been the father of organization theory, proposing a grouping of people into manageable numbers. The great armies of the world also organized into manageable numbers; soldiers wanted to follow the lead of the general, but not everyone could talk to the general. Officers were needed in

---

*Exodus - Chapter 18; Verses 15-23.

between. If you are directing soldiers' activities in war, you will want your word to be heard unequivocally and will want to hear questions of interpretation so the directive may be understood. The lines of authority that you establish, therefore, will be rigid, direct and central, emanating only from you.

Under most circumstances, people may try to interject some of their own ideas. Consequently it is necessary to standardize and develop specific rules and regulations. It also makes sense to utilize people with varying talents and skills to the best advantage of all. So historically we have learned to group people in manageable numbers, identify and maintain central authority, develop uniformity, and segregate specialized abilities. In the literature of managing, these methods are called classical organization theory. The theory is certainly valid, judging from the thousands of years these methods have been used. However, they are not as universally appropriate as their application in our organizations may indicate and many of us believe they should be drastically modified.

At the risk of oversimplifying the complexity of changes in the relationships among people in the last 100 years, it does seem that our ability to communicate with one another, especially technically, has significantly influenced the manner in which we should organize our associations of people. Obviously, if the only means of communication is running or riding a horse or camel, organizing will be much different from what it can be if one person can talk directly to another person thousands of miles away, and even see that person's image as they talk, as it is now possible to do. We watched and heard astronauts on the moon. We have computers that assemble and in a short time interpret data that a legion of information analysts could not do in a long time. The answers for new forms of association are not clear yet, but manager-leaders must be aware there are problems with the traditional forms.

A basic belief we have held about human behavior is that people tend to respond the way they think you want them to respond. There is pressure in a suggestion from you, because of your authority. If they think you want them to stay in a particular group they will tend to stay there and not interact or communicate with other groups. If they think you want to make all the decisions and do not want them to make decisions, they will not make them. If they think you are interested only in their special talents and skills, they may not show you that they have other abilities. If they think you want uniformity, they will not show you innovation. Traditionally, we have been ingrained with the admonition that we should do what we are told.

The traditional way of organizing people has also emphasized the impersonal aspects in the association of people. Followers have been inert instruments to be used in the most efficient and effective manner. Traditional methods have attempted to prevent individuality from disrupting the neatness and orderliness of the system. Followers were asked to perform in specific ways that the manager had decided for them. Managers have asked for conformity and relegated people to the system. Their goal was not to restrain followers but to achieve specialization, uniformity and central decision-making.

Throughout history, however, managers have been puzzled because their followers have done things that they really haven't been expected to do. While it is true that people generally tend to respond to their environment as they think they're supposed to, they also may respond on occasion as they want to, or as they must according to the dictates of their conscience.

These occasions have been multiplying. We are at a time when we must give wholly new consideration to the way manager-leaders interact with their followers. It is a tragedy when a person's sense of worth is eroded, when he or she becomes so confined and constricted by impersonal influences that there is no real idea of what might have been. We are coming to an age when people are no longer willing to accept the condition that what they do may depend more on the influences around them than on themselves. We are what we do, and I don't think we like what we have been doing.

If manager-leaders begin to recognize now that it is not only people's behavior with which they must deal but also, and more importantly, their capacity or potential, they will search more for what people can do and less for what they are doing. The time has come to implement the new relationships that seem to hold the promise of improvement.

If people are created equal, they certainly don't end that way. People do not want to be treated as equals if they are entitled to a greater share, nor do people want to receive less than their fair share. Followers are demanding their fair share of influence as a human right. It is not a question of whether or not you should allow yourself to be influenced by your followers, but how much influence you should allow in a given situation. Willingness to be influenced is practical. We have looked at the revolt against arbitrary management. If we wish to be successful, it is practical for us to do something about arbitrariness. The process of managing and leading is the process of decision-making, and so the influence that we allow our followers will be an influence in the decision-making process.

Sharing the decision-making process is extraordinarily practical in two ways. First, it gives us the advantage of the unique talents and perspectives of our followers. Two heads are better than one. The decision based on more and better information will be a better one. Secondly, when your followers obtain a responsible share in creating the conditions in which they will function, when you develop consensus, you interject the properties of conformity and cohesiveness which exert pressures in the association of your followers. Your job is easier when others help you.

Examine your own attitudes. How do you look at your relationship with your manager-leader? What do you hope for in it? What would you change tomorrow if you could? Most people with whom I talk want their manager-leaders to hear them out, to give them an opportunity to offer ideas and make suggestions based on what they know about their jobs. Are these your feelings? Do you really think your followers have such different feelings?

How do you let your followers influence you? Where do you start? Followers who have not made decisions with you before need to develop their ability and confidence. To give your followers a full measure of influence right away is to ask for confusion and chaos; they're simply not ready for it.

There are degrees of participation. Return to the "How to be more effective" section in Chapter One. Re-examine the degrees of participation from management to leadership.

Start slowly, not hastily. Be ready to discover that you may fail, that your followers may want more influence than they can handle, or that they won't think they can handle what you are sharing with them. It will be a struggle, but no one ever said it was easy. We find it difficult to break from our authoritarian training: "If it doesn't work, use more authority." Remember the discussion on authority, and keep in mind where final authority really rests.

Here are three warnings: First, don't attempt to interact with your followers in a superficial manner, attempting to give them a "feeling" of participation in the decision-making process but not a real opportunity to influence it. In other words, don't just go through the motions; it won't work. Followers know when they are being used. Second, participation in the decision-making process is not a panacea.

I believe participation is a better than average way for you to interact with your followers, but it in no way sets aside what we have said earlier, that managing and leading is an adaptive and relative process. Participation is not always appropriate; your firm hand will be required at times to push followers toward specific and definable goals. You could hardly be expected to practice participatory methods in an emergency.

The third warning is simply a reminder. Your final responsiblity is to make a decision. You can delegate the right to make some decisions to your followers, but some decisions must ultimately be made by you. You can't sidestep issues; when the time comes for a decision, you and you alone must make it.

Being open to influence is the new kind of relationship which manager-leaders must develop with their followers, searching for success in productivity, morale and job satisfaction. Examine the implications of sharing the influence to decide what happens next. We must break from the rigidness of what a few people think to the innovation of what many people can conceive. We're idea hunting, through people, to be as successful as possible in getting things done. Think about your responsibilities and your objectives. Think about the talents and skills of your followers. Think about suggestions they've made or questions they've asked. Where can they help? Where do they want to help? What can you share with them?

## How to be more effective

Return again to the improvement exercise in Chapter One. Instead of recording the way that you interact with your followers, use the scale to re-consider each management-leadership opportunity carefully and determine how much you are now willing to be influenced by your followers.

While you now know that each situation must be examined for its own dynamics—you may have to be a tough manager—you also know that finding ways to lead will gain you more success in the long run. Look at every situation. Eliminate ineffective approaches. Find the posture that seems most comfortable. Then look one notch toward leadership. Would it be a better way?

Listen to your followers.

Help them explore options. Help followers find a belief in the common purpose.

Teach them. Strengthen them. Inspire them. Help them learn and grow.

# Chapter Eight

# Human behavior always has some determining cause

Behavior is more than a form of action, a response to a stimulus, our active conduct. If we do nothing, we are still behaving. You cannot stop behaving; your existence is behavior. "Should I act (behave) in this situation?" is not a valid question. *"How* shall I act (behave) in this situation?" is the only question you face.

You think, you reason, you decide what you want to do and how you want to do it. People are, for the most part, conscious, rational, decision-makers. They face choices, examine and consider these choices, and decide which choice they want to accept.

Let's look at a model of human behavior which I have found helpful (see figure). The starting point is an initiator, whether an internal or external stimulus. We exclude physiologic behavior such as a reflex or heartbeat and psychopathic behavior, over which we rarely exercise voluntary control. When we are presented with an initiator, it is either known to us or it is not. If the initiator is unknown, that is, if we are unconscious or unaware of it, we will behave without thinking about what we are doing. We have values, attitudes, feelings, emotions, prejudices and biases, which influence our behavior in unexplainable ways.

Usually we are aware of the initiator, and we can either accept or reject it. One portion of behavior that is often confused with unconscious behavior and that I call explainable stems from a known initiator that is not recognized at a particular time. We are influenced, we behave, but we don't understand what we have done until we stop and think about it, or perhaps examine it with someone else, at some later time. Unconscious and explainable behavior constitute a small portion of behavior.

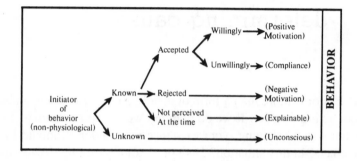

When we look at a known initiator, we often have the choice to accept or to reject it. We may choose not to eat, for example, but of course if we make the choice we will not live very long. One of your followers may choose to reject your suggestion, or initiator, to perform a certain activity. Your follower will behave, although not in the way you intended. I call this negative motivation, a negative response to the initiator.

Compliance behavior results from a known initiator which allows little or no choice. A choice has to be made, and we have the right to make a choice, but we aren't going to like any outcome. You may ask one of your followers to do something, and he or she may do it, even though he or she would rather not. The follower unwillingly accepts, complying with your request or direction. The tricky differentiation between compliance behavior and negative motivation has confused many manager-leaders. In both circumstances the known initiator is undesirable, but in compliance, the undesirability is not obvious. Thus you may mistake compliance for a willing, or positive response. Positive motivation is contrasted to undesired compliance; it is behavior which we willingly perform, something we want to do, something we like. An initiator presents itself, or is presented to us; we perceive it favorably, and we behave according to it. It's the kind of behavior we hope to get from our followers.

Compliance usually has to be induced each time the behavior is desired. This is tedious and time consuming for a manager-leader, something like manipulating a puppet. When you want action, you pull a string. If you don't pull a string, you will not get the action. Positive motivation is a wholly different way of managing and leading. People naturally tend to do things they enjoy, find rewarding, and think are valuable. Continual reminders for certain behavior become unnecessary.

We cannot expect each follower willingly to perform every act we ask. We have already asked the question: How do we resolve the conflicting needs of the people who are the association? It is unrealistic to think we can resolve all conflicts. It is, however, realistic to search for better ways to understand the needs which people bring to an association, and for better ways to meet them.

I consider the needs of the people to be the basis of behavior, the initiators. What is motivation? Motivation is the response to a need, an internal force or pressure within a person. Motivation is not an external stimulation. Motivation is not something you do to a person; you can't motivate people.

Humans are rational animals who choose among alternatives. They may choose to reject your external influence. If people behave according to your influence, but unwillingly, you have not "motivated" them as some people have thought of it, but you have induced them to comply with your influence. "Motivated" people, we have mistakenly said to ourselves, are those who enthusiastically do what *we* want them to do; "unmotivated" people do what *they* want to do.

What influences a person to choose among alternative initiators, alternative needs? Let's remind ourselves that the study of human behavior, human motivation, and human needs is complex, and that there is no clear answer to this question. However, we do have some substantial, though not universal, ideas about answers.

The effect of environment or other people on a person is the socio-dynamic influence which we have already examined. The psycho-dynamic influence is the individual's frame of reference, or personal perception of his or her existence. Frame of reference includes the past, or what a person has been and done; the present, or what he or she currently faces; and the future, or expectation of what lies ahead. We know where we have been, we partially know where we are, and we do not know where we will be.

We rely heavily on our experience to decide what to do, because that information is more certain and secure than our assessment of the present or our expectations of the future. The outcome of past assessments and expectations is known, and we tend to behave now as we have learned to behave in the past. This behavior pattern is called the law of effect. Unfortunately, it is not really a law, because we have all seen instances of behavior that completely contradicts what has been learned in the past. The effect is thus a tendency but not a law. People are just perverse enough to try something different.

Psycho-dynamic also includes a principle of reinforcement: Behavior that has been rewarded in the past tends to be continued, and behavior that has been punished in the past tends to be avoided. But the words "tends to" are important: If you believe a reward today will induce the same behavior tomorrow, you have made a serious mistake. There are some basic warnings about the reinforcement principle: Who considers the reward a reward? You, or your followers, or both? If your followers don't perceive a reward as a reward, why should they work for it? Do they consider the size of the reward a sufficient return for their effort? Are they convinced the kind of behavior you are rewarding should be rewarded? The belief that a person's actions always have pleasure as their purpose is not universal, although it makes sense, and it is generally correct to believe people will seek rewards and avoid punishments.

As children grow from immaturity to maturity, we observe a development from dependence to independence. We see selfish children become unselfish. We see a disregard for consequences turn into a serious concern, a lack of self control develop into self confidence, a refusal to accept responsiblity develop to a search for responsibility, wishful thinking turn into creative problem-solving, show-off tendencies become controlled behavior, destructiveness become constructiveness. We see these trends so often that we may believe all human beings develop this way. They don't, and certainly not by or at the age of 21, or whenever your state law says they become responsible adults. Human beings develop at different rates, and while a great many of them are emotionally mature by the age of 21, some of them are mature earlier, but some take much longer, and some remain immature.

Emotional maturity is not one concept, however. I mentioned eight separate aspects of emotional immaturity (not an inclusive list), which may develop at different rates; for example, a person may have learned the necessity for accepting responsibility for his or her own actions at age 14 but be unable to subdue show-off tendencies at age 54. Moreover, even though a person has learned to accept responsibility for his actions, he will not faithfully accept responsibility for all his actions throughout his life. A person who has learned the regard for consequences may nevertheless take risks, a person who has learned self control may lose that control, a person may engage in wishful thinking or simply destroy something in order to vent aggressiveness or hostility. Human beings are not perfect or perfectable.

The ethic that work is considered a virtue directed much of our life style. It prescribes hard work, purposeful activities, no leisure. The ethic has been challenged dramatically in the last generation or so: expressive or seemingly useless behavior, or leisure, is not only acceptable but necessary. We might ask: "What's wrong with just being myself?"

In the United States, we must add two other life-style directives: the American heritage and the capitalistic system. We are told to strive toward self reliance, responsibility, courage, new frontiers, individualism, profits. They may be appropriate for some people, but they are not universally appropriate. Our founding fathers didn't decree them for everyone; they declared that all men are endowed with the inalienable rights of life, liberty and the pursuit of happiness. I have met people who were happy being quite common, who willingly accepted the lead of others, who were not bad people because they did not have the courage to stand up and risk their lives in the defense of freedom, who could not compete and win at the expense of someone else's livelihood. The United States was founded on the principle of individual rights, but for some reason it has taken us 200 years to recognize and respect true individuality. Up to now, we have asked people to pursue their happiness in a collective way, through "our" happiness. We have come to think of a human being as one entity, somehow lumping what he does and what he is capable of doing into one perception. We behave a certain way in a given situtation, but we also have the capacity for other behavior.

The association of people has tendencies for both equilibrium and growth. The same tendencies exist in individuals. There is no, as has sometimes been thought, only a tendency for equilibrium, or only a tendency for growth, but there are rather tendencies for both. In much of the early writing on psychology there was an inordinate direction toward adjustment and the correction of deficiencies in human behavior—that is, toward equilibrium. Later thinking in psychology brought a dramatic emphasis on growth. There is plenty of room for both influences in our discussion: striving behavior—that is, coping, achieving, trying; and being-becoming behavior—that is, existing, growing, self actualizing. We have to understand these behaviors; we have to know about the needs which produce them.

We always need. One need, when satisfied, is followed by another need. When a second need is gratified, a third need presents itself. Needs come and go, their gratification is temporary. Once a need is satisfied, it will reappear for gratification later. The development of the intensity of each need toward gratification varies, one need from another (see figure). Our need to sleep, for example, presents itself approximately every 24 hours, although it may vary depending on the previous gratification, when we may have slept more or less than usual. The need for companionship may present itself a few times a day when we will want to be with other people, but at other times the same need may present itself only once in a few days. Our attempts to be precise about needs have been silly.

Our behavior is primarily organized around unsatisfied needs, although we are not helpless victims of them, having to respond at once when they appear. However, we can plan for unsatisfied needs and respond within our ability to predict when they will develop and require gratification. Needs do not always require complete gratification, but they will present themselves again sooner when they have been gratified only incompletely.

Gratifying a need does not always mean enjoying the gratification. We may be hungry, and we will eat to sustain ourselves, but we may not enjoy the food that is available. We may have a need to secure our future by working for money, but we are not required to enjoy the kind of work we do for the money we need. It is simplistic to follow a leadership philosophy which implies that need satisfaction means job satisfaction.

The humanistic psychologist Abraham Maslow was instrumental in giving us a perception and categorization of human needs that has clarified our understanding of them. By no means did he claim to be exhaustive in his discussion of them, but he has given us a start, and we must continue to learn. Our examination here will provide only a foundation for understanding this complex subject. It is not an explicit restatement of Maslow's theory, nor of anyone else's who has spoken on the subject.

I have found value in looking at needs arranged as shown

in the figure. The first grouping is physiologic, the basic body requirements, namely, food, water, air, rest, temperature control, bodily elimination. The second category of needs is security, to be free from fear, especially of physical danger or physiologic deprivation; to preserve oneself, clothe oneself, obtain shelter and safety for an extended period of time.

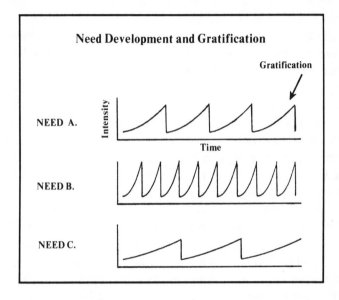

In the United States, money is as important a need as many of the others we are examining, although it is not usually classified among the other basic needs. Money is a medium of exchange for which we can obtain gratification of some other needs. Money has been a bad word in the management-leadership literature. When we began to question reward motivation, especially money, some people made the mistake of throwing the entire concept out with the dirty wash water. But money is essential if we are going to survive in our economy. However, researchers have proved beyond all question that people work for more than just money, that a variety of other needs may take precedence. More frequently than not, people stay at their employment because other needs they bring to the work environment are being gratified. Early in my career, I remember talking to a woman on a production line about her job and about the people with whom she worked. She said to me: "I like working here. I like the people I work with, and I like my foreman. You know as well as I do that I can walk two blocks down the street and get a job packing cookies for more pay."

A fourth category of needs includes those satisfied by other human beings, our association or social needs: the need to belong to a group; to be accepted, loved, wanted; to have the respect of others; to have companions. The last grouping is individual self-esteem or ego needs. Self-esteem needs are for respect, status, prestige, accomplishment, responsibility, freedom, independence, significance and personal growth.

All these needs, we believe, are in all people at all times, but they are different in general for each person and specifically for each person at a certain time. For example, we know people who generally have a high need to associate frequently with other people but specifically, even these people will sometimes, want to be alone.

## Categorization of Needs

| Physiologic | Security | Money | Association | Self-Esteem |
|---|---|---|---|---|
| Food<br>Water<br>Air<br>Rest<br>Temperature<br>Elimination | Preserve<br>Oneself<br>Avoid fear<br>Shelter<br>Safety | To buy the<br>things<br>necessary to<br>satisfy other<br>needs | Love<br>Companionship<br>Respect<br>Status | Prestige<br>Accomplishment<br>Responsibility<br>Freedom<br>Growth |

**Hierarchy of Prepotency**

Another aspect of this model will help us understand why our followers do or say some of the things they do. There is a pattern to the manner and succession in which our needs present themselves, or as Maslow said, a "hierarchy of relative prepotency." Our basic needs are physiologic—we must satisfy them before we can attempt to satisfy security, association or self-esteem needs. As physiologic needs are satisfied, we are free to concern ourselves with ensuring our security and well-being on a longer term basis. When we have farmed and hunted so we have enough food, when we have built some shelter for ourselves, when we have protected ourselves from wild animals, a new spectrum of needs will emerge—those of assocation, wanting to be with other human beings. We will form groups. Eventually, we will look to ourselves, to our self-esteem, our existence, what we are doing with ourselves, what we are achieving.

The general tendency is that unless the lower needs are gratified we will not seek to gratify higher needs. It is true, therefore, that when our lower order needs are threatened, we will sacrifice the fulfillment of higher needs. We are not likely to concern ourselves with a need to belong to a group if our security and survival as an individual is threatened.

Recognizing the validity of Maslow's "prepotency of human needs," however, we should not fall into the trap of thinking human beings are always predictable. You and I have known people who have not conformed to this succession. If the need to survive is so important, why have people given up their lives for principles of freedom? Why do some followers decide to stay with their groups when they could have better paying jobs, or more responsible jobs, somewhere else? The hierarchy of human needs tells us that if followers are quite secure about the future, if they have personal savings, enough medical and life insurance, and are now concentrating on the development of their personal abilities, we shouldn't offer them more security. Security rewards would not be an inducement. Instead, we should recognize and support their self-esteem needs.

Don't let me oversimplify the process of identifying and satisfying human needs. Perhaps it's sophomoric to say that human needs and their satisfaction are anything but simple, and yet I find leaders frequently overwrought, searching for answers in their attempts to understand another human being. Let's be realistic. There are some people whose needs can never be gratified in the normal sense, people who suffer a variety of psychiatric disorders, mental or emotional deficiencies, or functional disorders. Perhaps some of these people will be your followers, and you will be hard-pressed to deal with their cynicism, authoritarianism, prejudice, hatred, greed, guilt, insecurity, anxiety or fear, much less depressions, compulsions, phobic reactions, or schizophrenic behavior. We're not certain therapists know what to do about some of these either, but they are the only people who are competent to try.

As you continue your reading about human needs you will discover many surveys which describe needs of groups of people. What we have said about human beings in general will apply to your followers, but you must learn the specifics of your situation. Start looking at your followers' needs.

There are some specifics about the satisfaction of work needs with which you should be familiar. Job satisfaction is very much a personal perception, an extension of one's self image. Who we think we are and who we think we ought to be are our tests of the appropriateness of the kind of work we do and the place we do it. There are no simple answers to job satisfaction, but we can point to a variety of influences which have had a measurable effect on some people.

Choosing a particular occupation, a particular role in life, has an impact. How does your follower feel about his or her choice of occupation? How do other people—family and friends—feel about it? Were education, training and availability of assignments factors in selecting the occupation, rather than just the personality of the individual? Wouldn't one of your followers be secretly resentful if he or she had planned to work in a particular occupation but couldn't, for a variety of reasons, and was now working for you?

How do promotional opportunities, or the lack of them, affect your followers' job satisfaction? Where can they go, how can they prepare themselves, when can they be promoted? These are some of the influences which affect your followers' satisfaction, performance, motivation, behavior and needs. Not separately, but totally, they influence the whole person who follows your lead. Getting to know another human being, his or her standards of satisfaction and performance, kinds and intensity of needs, feelings and emotions, is at once the simplest and yet most complex task a manager-leader faces.

## How to be more effective

When you are disappointed in another person's behavior, and you have to talk about it:

> Stick to the facts—what your follower did
> Be specific about what actually happened
> Be accurate, not "you always..."
> Do not use derogatory words, or labels
> Do not talk about the follower's character
> Talk about one incident at a time
> Never talk about it when you are angry—be angry, by yourself, and then talk about

When you want a follower to change behavior:

> Be specific about what you want
> Be specific about what you do not want
> Ask for a small change
> State the consequences of no change
> Check whether or not you have to change, too

# Chapter Nine

## Don't judge by what they do, but what they can do

How do you recognize and understand human needs? Let's take a little mystery out of the process. You can learn just so much from reading books and talking to others about human needs, human motivation, and human behavior. You are already old enough, experienced enough, and wise enough to know most of

what you need to know about other people. What may be needed now is a reordering of what you have already experienced. Let's go through some exercises to provide a basis for understanding other human beings. Here first is a series of questions I'd like you to answer.

1. What is the first thing you see in the ink blot?
2. How tall, in feet and inches, is a "tall" man?
3. What is the population of a "small" town?
4. If you have an appointment at 9 a.m., how many minutes would be considered arriving too early? Too late?
5. If the speed limit posted is 30 m.p.h., how many m.p.h. over the limit should a motorist be allowed before being stopped for speeding? How many m.p.h. under the limit before being stopped for driving too slowly?
6. What color do you consider most relaxing?
7. In considering a fair day's work, what percentage of the hours worked in a day (excluding rest periods) should a person be working productively?
8. How many absences for short-term illness or personal reasons per year are excessive for an employee?
9. How much pain is enough to make a person groan?

Let's consider some answers I've heard in personal discussions. For the first question, What is the first thing you see in the ink blot?, I have heard these responses: some images, two monks, carrots, cut flower, grotesque, two birds, a man with his arms over his head, two leaves, flowers, footprint, male and female aging. The most frequent response is butterfly.

How tall, in feet and inches, is a "tall" man? 5'8", 5'10", 6', 6'1", 6'2", 6'3", 6'4", 6'5", 6'6", 6'7", 6'10", 7'4", 7'6", 10' and "as tall as they feel."

What is the population of a "small" town? 10, 50, 100, 300, 400, 500, 1,000, 1,500, 2,500, 5,000, 10,000, 15,000, and 50,000.

If you have an appointment at 9 a.m., how many minutes would you consider arriving too early? 1, 10, 15, 20, and 30. Arriving too late? 1, 3, 5, 10, and 30.

If the speed limit posted is 30 miles per hour, how many miles over the limit should a motorist be allowed before being stopped for speeding? 0, 1, 5, 6, 10, over 33 miles per hour, "allowing 10 per cent variance of odometer and variances of foot."

How many miles per hour under the limit before being stopped for driving too slowly? 0, 5, 8, 9, 10, 15, 20, 25 and "it depends."

What color do you consider most relaxing? Green, light green, greenish blue, blue, sky blue, soft blue, light blue, pale blue, yellow, brown, beige, white, skin color, depends on the season, and Southern Comfort (whiskey).

In considering a fair day's work, what percentage of the hours worked in the day (excluding rest periods) should a person be working productively? 70, 75, 80, 87, 7/8, 90, 93, 95, 97, 100, 110, and "depends on the person's job."

How many absences for short-term illness or personal reasons per year are excessive for an employee? 3, 5, 7, 10, 12, 15, 20, 25, 30 and "there are no excesses."

How much pain is enough to make a person groan? Depends on where the pain is inflicted; not very much; any pain of nagging or throbbing tendencies; slamming your head in a door; any, when it really hurts; don't know; and, "it's different for each individual."

What's the point of these questions and the variety of answers? Think about the implications of what your opinion, as opposed to the different opinions of other people, means to you. In the first exercise, were you impressed with the array of opinions expressed? I was. So many different thoughts about the same thing! Shouldn't some of the answers have been more obvious? Perhaps you're puzzled because you have what you felt was a sensible answer, yet other people gave different reasons. Didn't they think their answers were just as sensible? Perhaps you thought your answer might be the most sensible answer.

We act according to our perceptions. Our actions are based either on reality or on assumptions, but how easy it is to mistake the two! In a philosophical sense, we can argue that there is no certainty, and we must make assumptions in order to act. It is not a question of whether or not we will assume, but how well founded our assumptions are. We are capable of being considerably more precise about reality than we have been. We have all been caught in our assumptions, especially about people—in our expectations about their answers to the questions in our exercise, for example—but we improve only rarely. Yet we must improve if we are going to be more effective manager-leaders.

The concept which has made the most sense to me about assessing the reality of human behavior is that people's behavior makes sense *to them.* Do you behave in a way that doesn't make sense to you? I doubt it. But do we allow other people the same right about their behavior? How frequently have you and I said, "What a stupid thing to do!"

Accepting the word "sensible" is not easy. Some people stretch our ability to even say the word. Champion chess players have argued over chess boards that were too shiny, too light in color, too large or too small. Sensible? Certainly, if you are playing a world championship.

Although we do not usually encounter the following kind of behavior, I wonder if we can use it to illustrate my point about the difficulty in accepting what is and is not sensible. A newspaper reported that a young man was murdered on an elevated train. The story said:

"At one point the student left his seat and walked to the front of the car, to avoid the four youths, the witness told the police.

"They followed him, sitting in seats around the one he chose, the witness said, and continued to harass him.

"Finally, one of the four asked, 'Shall we pop him? to which another is said to have responded, 'Yeah, pop him.'

"One of the youths then shot (the student)...."

Sensible? We could speculate on the mental stability of at least the one youth who actually committed the murder. Perhaps he had some mental disorder, but more frequently we find, even in these cases, that no disorder is present; only, disastrously, a warped value system.

When sales clerks ignore us, do you think they consider their behavior sensible? When drivers run a red light across your path, do you think they consider their behavior sensible? When people walk into a meeting late, do you think they consider their behavior sensible?

We are trying to understand something about human behavior, human motivation, and human needs. While we may be pressed to our limits, we need to work all the harder to accept the word sensible when we think of the behavior of other people, not sensible *to us,* but sensible *to them,* for whatever reasons. If we do not, there is absolutely no opportunity for us to see the other person's point of view. If we cannot see the other person's point of view, how can we ever begin to work productively with that person? We can't.

If we look at a person's behavior and say: "He shouldn't have done that," we may be absolutely correct, but we seem to get hung up on what the person shouldn't have done, not what can be done to improve behavior. We're denying reality. We end up with two problems: the behavior "he shouldn't have committed," which still exists, and secondly, our own psychological denial of reality, which must be overcome.

I'm not asking you to agree on what behavior is right or wrong. The question of values is an entirely different question. We are looking only at a person's behavior from the point of view of what makes sense to him. We are not asking whether he knows right from wrong, only what he may consider as sensible, justifiable, reasonable or logical at the time, given the surrounding circumstances, environment, and his perception of life's pressures.

We have an image of ourselves, made up of what we think we are and what we think we ought to be. We want to maintain but also enchance ourselves, find an equilibrium but also grow. We are the center of our own psychological world, and it is usually only our perception of our world that matters greatly to us. The opinion of others usually does not induce us to change. We rationalize that other people ought to change. People want to be themselves and management and leadership will be an impossible process if followers want to be someone other than the manager-leader wants them to be.

The impact of assumptions we make about other people, especially assumptions manager-leaders make about followers, was emphasized by Douglas McGregor. This concept is, I believe, a most important contribution to the process of managing and leading. McGregor didn't just dream up assumptions about people. As he talked to many manager-leaders, he noted implicit assumptions about human nature and human behavior in their managerial strategies, decisions and actions. McGregor believed there were many sets of beliefs about human nature and human behavior which a manager-leader could hold about his or her subordinates. Two of these sets of beliefs were called Theory X and Theory Y.* Theory X is the traditional view of direction and control. Its tenets are: (1) The average human being has an inherent dislike of work and will avoid it if possible; (2) because of this human characteristic of dislike of work, most people must be coerced, controlled, directed or threatened with punishment to get them to put forth adequate effort toward the achievement of organizational objectives, and (3) the average human being prefers to be directed, wishes to avoid responsibility, has relatively little ambition, wants security above all.

Theory Y, on the other hand, McGreogor called the integration of individual and organizational goals. Theory Y is not the polar opposite of Theory X on a continuum but an altogether different set of beliefs: (1) The nature of mental and physical effort in work is as natural as play or rest; (2) external control and the threat of punishment are not the only means of bringing about ef-

---

*McGregor, Douglas: "The Human Side of Enterprise," New York: McGraw-Hill Book Company, 1960, pp. 33-34, 47-48. Readers may also be interested in McGregor's other work, "The Professional Manager" (McGraw-Hill, 1967).

fort toward organizational objectives; man will exercise self-direction and self-control in the service of objectives to which he is committed; (3) commitment to objectives is a function of the rewards associated with their achievement; (4) the average human being learns, under proper conditions, not only to accept but to seek responsibility, and (5) the capacity to exercise a relatively high degree of imagination, ingenuity and creativity in the solution of organizational problems is widely, not narrowly, distributed in the population; under the conditions of modern industrial life, the intellectual potentialities of the average human being are only partially utilized.

The assumptions we make about human beings are complex and have created much discussion and interpretation about what McGregor did or did not say. For me, he seemed to argue for the acceptance of Theory Y and yet his arguments were not one-sided. As Edgar Schein said in the introduction to "The Professional Manager," "Few people have acknowledged that McGregor's book made a netural point about the examination of one's assumptions, the testing of them against reality, and then the selection of a managerial strategy that made sense in terms of one's diagnosis of reality."

I have found it helpful to differentiate two points of view about human beings: their behavior—what they do, and their capacity—what they can do. Because of the contrasting nature of Theory X and Theory Y, for the moment let's put them at opposite ends of a continuum of belief about human beings, but let's make one continuum for behavior and another for capacity (see diagrams).

When we consider the behavior of one of our followers, we must respond to the reality of the behavior exhibited. A person may act lazily at a particular moment or may not; may show a dislike for work at a moment or may not; may prefer to be directed at a moment, or may not. Management and leadership as we have examined it is an adpative and relative process. It would be absurd to ignore a follower's need for direction at a particular time

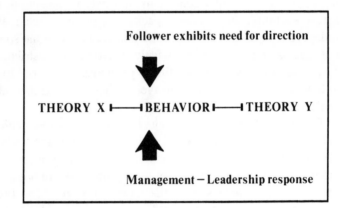

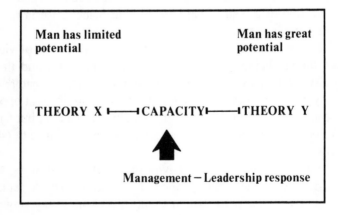

when we are trying to get something done through that follower.
If we do not respond to his or her need for direction a follower
will either do nothing or do something other than what we intended.

On the other hand, considering human capacity is a totally
different perception. The continuum from X to Y turns out to be
a bad to good contrast. I personally don't see how we can view
people in any other capacity than Theory Y, their potential to function well and effectively, to grow. We short-change our followers and ourselves if we believe anything but Theory Y. At a
particular moment a follower may need direction, but one moment is not a lifetime.

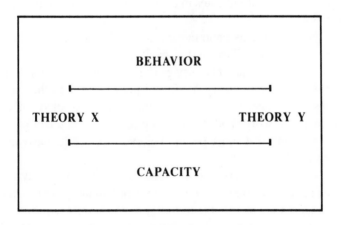

The confusion that I hear in discussions about human beings stems from making no distinction between people's behavior
and their capacity. Unknowingly, arguments jump from one perception to another. McGregor was asked to choose a managerial
strategy that made sense in terms of our diagnosis of reality, which
means to me that we must respond appropriately to the behavior

that is presented to us. At the same time, but from a completely different point of view, McGregor believed in the possibility of human growth and development, and the unlimited capacity of people.

What assumptions do you hold about people? I think it would be a worthwhile exercise to stop and examine your thoughts. What do you think about the way people will or should act that guides you in the decisions you make about them? How well do they align with the sets of assumptions McGregor presented? Which view of people's capacity do you think most generally describes people today?

Answers I have heard have shifted over the years from leaning toward Theory X to leaning toward Theory Y. I think the shift is good, because it indicates that we are beginning to believe more in people.

Now let me ask another question: Which theory, X or Y, more closely describes your capacity?

Theory Y is the only answer I've ever heard. Nearly all people think they are Theory Y kind of people but the other person is closer to Theory X. I'm okay, but you're not okay. It's our self-image at work, and it's a strong feeling. When can we start understanding that other people believe they are just as capable as we think we are?

I don't like every human being I meet; I don't always want to see his or her point of view. But when I sit and listen to manager-leaders they tell me the darndest things about themselves and about the problems they are having with followers and other leaders. Often they are warm and open and witty. I want to get to know them. I've talked to groups of manager-leaders who tell me at length about the problems they are having with the manager-leader they work for. From the dicussion I could easily get the impression that the top manager-leaders are two-headed monsters. Yet when I sit with them I find people who are interested in doing their jobs, who want to be successful, who are not bad people. It's a humorous contrast and yet of course it is sad. It dramatically accents the assumptions we make about other human beings and the desperate need for us to be more open and understanding, to respect another person's point of view and self-image.

As much as I want you to think about the assumptions you make about other people, I am not overly confident major changes will occur immediately in your attitudes. Most of you have already defined the way you think about other human beings, and I do not deny your right to those beliefs. If your beliefs are perhaps a little narrow, I hope you may begin to consider new ways of thinking about people. I think of a success I had in a group discussion which made me particularly happy. The group consisted of approximately 15 industrial foremen who were participating in discussions of supervisory development on their own time. Their seniority as foremen ranged from 6 to 26 years. Some of the men were quite set in their ways. Yet they were willing to learn, and I admired them for that. We talked for many weeks about a variety of topics, mostly people problems. At the end, we tried to examine what we had gained from these discussions, and one foreman, who was about 60 years old and a pretty tough kind of guy, said he felt a little more interested in his employees, and in what they had to say. I remember his comment: "When an employee said something to me I just told him what I thought right away. Now, I take two steps back—before I tell him what I think."

A management-leadership strategy based on a growth of human capacity opens new vistas in relationships with followers. The satisfaction of man's lower order needs is basically an exercise in obtaining relief from a pretty dismal experience, but the satisfaction of the higher order needs is one of exciting possibilities. We are in the midst of a change in the way we organize for productivity. Industry, the most highly organized segment of American society, is feeling the most violent pangs of change. Employee frustration is reported weekly in newspaper accounts and business columns. Employees are tired of performing boring and meaningless tasks, tired of being constricted and forced into a daily lock step which doesn't make any sense to them or isn't what they want to do. They're not asking for the right of rejection, but they are asking for an opportunity to influence. They don't want to be consumed totally by their environment. And let's remember what we've already learned about the effect of an environment: Followers who perceive an environment as constricting may not show their capabilities for innovation. Don't be misled into thinking they aren't capable of innovation.

Working doesn't have to be an unhappy experience for most followers, and yet it is for many. Not all jobs are capable of being good jobs; some have become so routine that they are beyond improvement. Most jobs can be invigorating and need not drive a follower home to find refuge in a hobby, to find his or her mind again. Young people are shouting the loudest to be heard, but older people feel the same way. People know they have the capacity. We are still denying reality: They shouldn't do that; I don't know why they feel that way. The reality is that they *do* feel that way; their behavior is sensible to them. However, what they are really asking in a new relationship, not what they ask for after having been angrily provoked into undesirable behavior by our rejection, is no more than we usually ask of the people whom we follow.

Frederick Herzberg talked to employees and asked them what good and bad things happened to them on their jobs.* What kinds of things made them satisfied, and dissatisfied? Generally, he found such things as company policy and administration, supervision, working conditions, salary, relationships with peers, relationships with subordinates, status and security were factors that contributed to job dissatisfaction. On the other hand, elements of achievement, recognition, responsibility, advancement, growth and the job itself contributed to job satisfaction. The interesting observation is that the opposite of job dissatisfaction is not job satisfaction, but rather, no job dissatisfaction. If you do a good job of improving and main-

---

*Frederick Herzberg, Bernard Mausner, and Barbara Bloch Snyderman: "The Motivation to Work," New York: John Wiley & Sons, 1959. Also Herzberg, "Work and the Nature of Man," World Publishing Co., 1966.

taining factors such as company policy and administration, working conditions, security—that is, the hygiene factors—you will eliminate job dissatisfaction, but you will not necessarily make employees particularly satisifed with their jobs.

In order to help employees achieve satisfaction with their jobs, different influences must be brought into the job environment—namely, motivation factors such as achievement, recognition, responsibility, growth.

It's not an easy task to manage or lead people who are searching for freedom. It's a wholly new relationship. It's challenging and difficult, but very rewarding. Managers who only manage are controllers, checkers. They really don't know what it is to lead human beings and participate in human growth. We need a concern for other than the specifics of people working at their jobs; we need to think about the quality of their lives. We have asked people to sell themselves as tools in a materialistic society.

Today, followers respond to an environment which tells them to respond economically, narrowly, with little or no personal expression. Not all followers want to participate eagerly, nor do all followers seek to develop their minds, or seek growth, or try to improve interpersonal relationships. However, the rejection of these attributes by some followers, for whatever reasons, does not mean we should withhold this way of living from others. The lowest common denominator is no longer appropriate or necessary in our pursuit of effectiveness. We must learn to deal with multiple ways of relating and living. Some people say our manager-leaders have tried and rejected the concepts of behaviorists and humanists as unworkable. I say most manager-leaders have never really examined these concepts.

We're not talking about giving away the association to our followers and letting them do what they want with it, but we are attempting to recognize that our followers have much to contribute, more to contribute than we have asked or allowed. Followers are demonstrating their desire to contribute by their demands for change in society and in our institutions. They are not saying they reject a manager-leader authority, but they are reminding them where their authority originates. Followers are looking for equitable relationships with their manager-leaders and pointing to their right to this kind of relationship.

We have not studied enough about psychological health. Most of what we have learned about human beings has come from the study of psychologically sick people. The literature on management has been overly concerned with control, discipline, training and coping, trying to bring people into line. It has dealt with reward and punishment. We need to study the new richness of healthy human beings, to face the challenges of developing self-esteem. We need to move toward what we want to be, toward spontaneity, authenticity, naturalness and choice.

## How to be more effective

Many people are disgruntled because they don't feel good about themselves. People feel good when they have:

> Skill
> Influence
> Recognition
> Money

Maybe you can't address all of these needs, and maybe you can. What can you do to help each of your followers feel more valuable and productive? Ask yourself these questions:

> What skills can you help them develop?
> How can you help them influence their situation?
> How can you recognize their efforts?
> How can you help them earn more money?

# Chapter Ten

# Manager-leaders don't just talk, they must also listen

The classic failure in interpersonal communications is the failure to recognize the other person's right to believe in the good sense of his or her point of view. We have wanted our point of view to be accepted and the other point of view abandoned. It has been an I-win, you-lose battle. We have not exchanged information and values as much as we have talked at each other. The influence has been subtle, and devastating. I-win, you-lose is appropriate when the other person is wrong, but who among us, except rarely, has communicated well enough to say with certainty that they are right and the other person is wrong? We must begin instead to say: "I see the situation this way, and it seems sensible to me. You see the situation that way, and it seems sensible to you."

The basic model for examining communications between human beings involves two levels, content and feelings. Content is the surface communication, the more obvious, what is heard, seen, touched or smelled, the who, what, how, when, where. Feelings are below the surface, not so obvious, the emotions, values, needs or attitudes—harder to understand and deal with, more volatile, and more influential.

How many times have you talked with another person and walked away saying to yourself, "He or she never really understood me"? The other person didn't "hear" your feelings. How many times have you talked with another person and as you watched sensed that he or she had something else to say but wasn't saying it? Feelings were being hidden.

Where people associate, the policies and procedures have not caused as many problems as the feelings of the people who have expressed or argued about them. We need to deal with problems at their content level, to be sure, but more importantly, we need to deal with them at the level of feelings. Unfortunately, even when we recognize an expression of feelings, often we don't know what to do with them.

Let's begin with a look at the basic mechanical process of sending and receiving a message. A person (information source) who possesses some knowledge, opinion or attitude wants to express himself or herself to another person. He or she starts talking (encoding the message) and sends the message through sound waves (transmission) to another person who hears (reception) the message and interprets it for understanding (decoding). When you think of the process it looks simple, but I'm sure you can begin to sense the kinds of problems which can occur in just these few steps.

Let's try an exercise. I want you to think about, or discuss with friends, some barriers to communications. What barriers or problems have you experienced in listening and talking to other human beings? Think about it. Observe your conversations closely. Then we'll look at what other people have told me about the barriers they have experienced.

Other people have told me about these problems or barriers to effective listening and talking:

- People don't listen; they don't let you finish.
- People don't know how to get their ideas across.
- The listener may be distracted.
- There may be different levels of comprehension between the talker and the listener.
- Tone and inflection change the meaning of the words.

Other barriers to understanding that may be listed include:

- Physical speech or hearing impairment
- Emotional factors
- Language barrier
- Age difference
- Environmental differences
- Lack of common interest
- More concern with what I'm saying than with what the other person is saying
- Lack of concentration by listener or talker
- Message not stated clearly
- Thinking ahead to what you are going to say
- Preoccupation with another subject
- Poor speaking habits; monotonous, unorganized thoughts
- Insecurity or lack of confidence
- Poor attitude or lack of trust
- Disruptive physical environment
- Mood of the participants
- Saying one thing but meaning another
- Use of colloquialisms or jargon
- Being involved in a new situation; feeling tense
- Status differences
- Paying too much attention to "body language"
- Not paying enough attention to "body language"
- Defensiveness
- Cultural differences
- Bias, prejudice or stereotyping
- Wrong assumptions about people

To all these I would add the barrier of polarization, or looking at a situation as being either one way or the other. Some situations are either one way or the other, but others are not: A person is either 5'9" tall or not; a town either has a population of 15,243 or not; a person either has a particular disease or not. However, a person does not have to be either tall or short, he can be medium height; a town does not have to be either large or small, it can be medium size; a person is not healthy or unhealthy, there are degrees of healthiness.

In much the same way, followers are not either trained or untrained but are in the various states of preparedness; followers are not attentive or inattentive but will be in some state of attentiveness or inattentiveness at the moment; followers are not congenial or uncongenial but are congenial at some times and uncongenial at others; followers are not accurate or inaccurate but accurate about some things and not so accurate about others.

How do you overcome the barriers to communication? Start by recognizing that they exist. Take one or two of the more obvious problems, the ones that are particular sore spots, and concentrate on a program of improvement. Be attentive, watch your communications closely. Get help from wherever you can. Face reality; don't deny that barriers exist or rationalize that they shouldn't be there. Look to yourself first, before you try to solve the other person's problem.

Let's look at the common barriers to communications and consider a suggestion to correct or alleviate each one. There are many ways to approach each barrier, and I'm sure you will want to figure some of them out for yourself.

*Barrier:* People don't listen, they don't let you finish.

*Correction or alleviation:* How about tactfully asking if you could finish what you started to say—or—acknowledging that you wish to hear other comments but would like to present your side of the story also. Or—relax and let the other person wind down.

*Barrier:* There may be different levels of comprehension between the talker and the listener.

*Correction or alleviation:* If you are the talker and have the higher level of comprehension, the burden is on you to simplify your presentation, but by all means avoid talking down to your listener. Usually the talker and the listener have to work this problem out together, the one talking more simply, the other stretching his or her mind to understand.

*Barrier:* Inflection changes the meaning of the words.

*Correction or alleviation:* If you sense that a word's meaning has been changed, ask about it; apply the feedback principle: "Is this what you meant?"

*Barrier:* Emotional factors.

*Correction or alleviation:* Let the emotion run its course. When people are caught up emotionally in a situation, they want to let it all hang out. Don't try to interrupt.

*Barrier:* Age difference.

*Correction or alleviation:* Age itself is not a barrier. The barrier is a different perception of environment, the different connotation of a word. Exchange perceptions and connotations: "Do you mean...?"

*Barrier:* Lack of concentration by the listener or talker.

*Correction or alleviation:* If the problem is with you, start concentrating! Bear down on what's being said; examine words closely; find a reason to be interested. If the lack of concentration is in the other person, wait for another time when he or she is more willing to concentrate. Or pause when you see a lack of concentration, or ask questions now and then to test comprehension of what you have said and ask if there is any other information you might add. This signals that the other person is going to have to listen to avoid embarrassment.

*Barrier:* Thinking ahead to what you are going to say.

*Correction or alleviation:* This is another way of saying you're not listening. What good does it do to know what you are going to say later if you don't know what you are hearing now?

*Barrier:* Poor speaking habits, monotonous, unorganized thoughts.

*Correction or alleviation:* If it's your problem, perhaps a speech course at a local school or a Dale Carnegie course would be helpful. Think about what you want to say before you start talking; if necessary, write some notes or prepare an outline. Help other people who have these problems by asking questions to clarify the meaning of their message, or by tactfully pointing out some of their poor habits of speaking.

*Barrier:* Insecurity or lack of confidence.

*Correction or alleviation:* Lack of confidence is often only a matter of knowing your subject better. Do your homework before you enter conversations.

*Barrier:* Use of colloquialisms or jargon.

*Correction or alleviation:* Be aware that the words you use may not be understood by people in a different profession or from a different part of the country. Watch for puzzled looks and interpret. When you hear colloquialisms or jargon, stop the talker and ask for an interpretation.

*Barrier:* Status differences.

*Correction or alleviation:* Status itself isn't a barrier. The barrier is the person who either has or lacks the status. Be aware that status may impair the situation; for example, a person may feel awkward about asking a technical question that he or she thinks may appear stupid.

*Barrier:* Defensiveness.

*Correction or alleviation:* A person is defensive when he or she thinks there is something that should be protected or kept from you. Don't attack a defensive position, since only stronger defenses will result. Do the best you can to be relaxed and trustful.

*Barrier:* Cultural differences.

*Correction or alleviation:* These kinds of differences are difficult to counteract, because we usually don't know they exist. A culture is a way of living, and it is frequently difficult to understand differences until they are brought to our attention, when, for example, we might violate a custom. If you understand the concept of culture you are more than half way toward an appropriate alleviation of the problem. Talk carefully, and ask about things you don't understand.

*Barrier:* Bias, prejudice or stereotyping.

*Correction or alleviation:* Good information offers our only hope of overcoming this barrier. We have a barrier, usually, not because good information wasn't available, but because we have presented it argumentatively and challengingly to defeat the other person.

Perhaps your best opportunity for improvement in communicating is to develop your willingness and ability to listen. Much has been said and written about the way people can improve their listening habits. There are ways of organizing or looking at the ways people respond to us, or the ways we respond to them, that are helpful guides to improving our ability to communicate successfully. Here is one structure. (See box on page 99).

Criticizing is the lowest form of communicating, and listening is the highest, but each form of relating is absolutely appropriate, depending on the situation in which you find yourself. There is nothing wrong with avoiding, or giving orders, or asking if the particular response is apppropriate to what was said.

Listen to conversations, and examine your own, and categorize what people say. If you should find most responses at the lower levels, you will also find, as a result, that most communications are rather unsuccessful—a lot of content being heard but feelings being missed. You should find successful conversations resulting from the use of higher forms of relating, listening or agreeing or asking.

How many times have you had a person come to you for help with a problem. As they described the problem, for some reason you didn't respond, but just listened. Finally, the person said, "Thanks for helping me; I see a solution I didn't see before." You didn't say anything, but you listened. That's successful communication, in many cases.

A person feels accepted when you listen, when you are willing to see his or her point of view. No defense, no I-win, you-lose, is necessary. A person might be willing to receive some help with a problem, may even be willing to let you persuade, if you have listened. Listening provides the opportunity to close the communications system with feedback. Unless you have listened, you can hardly know how to respond.

The reflecting form of active listening warrants special attention because it is the most difficult, but probably the most helpful, form of responding. Reflecting is restating what a person has just said to you with perhaps a slight variation or attempt at interpretation. It is not repeating or parroting. Reflecting is an active way to help a person say what he or she really wants to say, what he or she is feeling, below the content of the message. You are trying to be "assumptionless" in your communicating effort, not presuming you know all of what the other person is trying to tell you.

Reflecting gives a person an opportunity to examine what he or she has said: "No, that's not what I meant," or, "Yes, that's it." For example, someone might say: "I don't know what to do." You could reflect: "You're puzzled." The person might respond by saying to you, "Yes, I am puzzled; I just haven't been able to get the information I need to have in order to make a decision."

When another person reflects your statements, you can examine your own thinking. You will hear your statements rephrased, and you will gain a slightly different perspective on your thinking.

Let's consider the influence of nonverbal communications. We have said that existence is behavior, and now we add, behavior is communications. Therefore, existence is a form of communication. You cannot stop behaving; you cannot stop communicating. When you stand still, doing and saying nothing, you are communicating. The way we act supports or denies what we say in words.

Don't be impressed with some of the popular works on nonverbal communications which suggest rigid or automatic indicators from body movements. The process of communications is complex, verbally and nonverbally. With some success, you can use the model for nonverbal communications as with verbal: People act out criticizing, avoiding, comforting and giving orders. For example, when I see a person's eyes become somewhat glassy and distant, I assume he or she is avoiding, not really paying attention to the conversation. When people read something while you are talking to them, they *are* avoiding. How often have you heard a person say he or she was sorry about something, but their actions were not consoling?

When a person hunches forward in a chair I get ready for some movement in the conversation, maybe agreeing, maybe a

**Listening**

I'd like to hear about it.
That's interesting.
Let's talk about it.

**Agreeing**

I agree with you.
You're right.

**Asking**

When did you start feeling this way?
What happened then?
Then what did he or she say?
How many times did you try?
Why do you say that?
How do you feel about that?

**Persuading**

You ought to.
Wait a little before you decide.
I suggest you talk to them first.
Look at it this way.
You have the ability.
Would you mind doing this first?

**Giving orders**

Do this first.
Deliver these papers.
Would you please have this prepared.

**Comforting**

I'm sorry to hear that.
I know, work can be pretty boring.
You'll feel differently tomorrow.
Don't worry, things will work out.

**Avoiding**

Just forget about it.
Let's not talk about it now.
What else is happening?

**Criticizing**

Stop complaining.
If you do that, you'll be sorry.
You're not thinking clearly.
I couldn't disagree with you more.
You really don't believe that, do you?
We've been through this before.

contradiction, or perhaps some persuading. Much nonverbal communications is reasonably obvious; you need only look for it.

Try to pick the time and circumstances of communicating if you can. Watch the timing of what you say; don't try any tricks; don't communicate when you're tired, busy, preoccupied or angry.

Several years ago I walked in a parade with a Cub Scout pack, and at the conclusion we gathered for a flag ceremony. There was to be soda and ice cream afterward for the children who had marched, and, naturally, they were waiting for the goodies before the ceremony began and were a bit noisy. One of the village fathers took a dim view of this "disrespect for our flag" and in a sweeping generalization began to indict young people who had lost their sense of American ideals. My temper flared, and at the conclusion of the ceremony I went forward to make my feelings known. Two young people had already cornered the speaker and were trying to explain themselves. As I approached, they sensed I was going to support them and they let me talk.

For all I have taught and coached about communications, I blew it. I was too angry and couldn't think clearly. Even as I heard the words as they came tumbling out, I couldn't stop and present a good argument. I certainly didn't change one iota of that man's attitude. In any event, I felt better.

Whenever I discuss communications, usually someone comments about a lot of other people, who need to learn something about communications. I always get uneasy then, because I'm fairly certain the person commenting can use the most improvement. Sooner or later, we must look at ourselves, and then, finally, we need to look at some of the special problems of communicating in an association of people.

There are three basic communications channels which manager-leaders can make available to their followers. First, a direct channel to first-level manager-leaders; second, an appeal system, or grievance procedure, to middle and upper-level manager-leaders; and third, a direct channel to the upper-level manager-leaders through an attitude survey.

First-line manager-leaders are in direct contact with most of the followers. They are in the critical middle, the point of conflict between upward and downward communications. They are the most important communicators in the association. The most obvious breakdown in a channel to them occurs because they have failed to make a psychological contract with themselves to listen to their followers, and consequently are unable to respond. The not so obvious reason for this communications breakdown is that upper-level manager-leaders do not listen and respond to what the first-line manager-leaders relay from their followers. The whole problem is one of upward communication, and it seems that our only response has been to try harder to correct the upward communication problems by increased or intensified downward communication.

If you examine the internal structure of most associations you will find an almost impossible situation, namely a hierarchy of too many levels. Communications are expected to be passed along from one level to the next. As in the game in which a story is whispered from person to person around a circle, when the first person and the last person both recite the story, the two are entirely different.

I said the first-level manager-leaders are the most important communicators, and in the long run, these manager-leaders must become better communicators if the association is going to be successful. But other ways of improving communications up and down the association structure are required if we're going to achieve our purposes.

The appeal system provides an alternative channel for followers who do not feel secure in discussing their needs with the manager-leaders, or who have not received satisfactory answers to their problems. Appeals are a necessary release mechanism for frustration and an essential adjunct to an environment of followers' satisfaction and association effectiveness. We have come to undersand that traditional organizational structures have subtly suggested, even demanded, rigid functional and interpersonal relationships. This is more obvious in larger organizations, but it is found in small ones as well. This rigidity has produced conflicts among people who are associated together, especially conflicts that result from protecting department protocols. People do not always cooperate, and it may well be the organization structure that inherently prevents the cooperation we have worked so hard to achieve. We want cooperation, but we also want organizational conformity. The two goals may be incompatible.

We cannot deny association conflict simply because it isn't supposed to exist. We know people will have problems, and they will talk about them. Small associations are quick to say they don't need a formal appeal system because everybody knows everybody else and knows what's going on. But by not formally agreeing to an appeal system, we implicitly say that the formal structure must be recognized, that it cannot be circumvented, and that decisions made by manager-leaders are to be followed and not appealed, even in the face of an injustice. In reality, we rarely demand such conformity. In essence, therefore, we officially recognize the formal structure but also allow the informal system to operate—a subtle inconsistency.

Followers will differ with their manager-leaders and they need a mechanism to appeal decisions to a higher level of the association. Manager-leaders who understand that they will make mistakes, even with the best of intentions and training, and who want to be successful and want to see opinions openly discussed and examined, will not resist an appeal system. They will welcome it.

The third channel which should be available to followers is an attitude survey—using a questionnaire and structural interview—in which each follower has an opportunity to express a personal opinion directly to upper-level manager-leaders regarding conditions in the association. The questionnaire provides a simple and inexpensive method to reach every follower in the association. The structural interview ensures detailed attention to all factors which affect the situation.

## How to be more effective

Some helpful hints when talking to your followers:

- Avoid contradicting
- Agree whenever you can
- Ask questions until you don't learn anything new
- State what you understand about what the other person said, or about what you agree to do
- Talk positively about what you want rather than what you don't want
- Time what you say
- Go back and pick up the pieces when conversations go bad
- Follow the rules—go to the person, verify the facts, and act promptly before emotions get out of hand

# Chapter Eleven

## How shall we evaluate our followers?

Performance appraisal measures how well our objectives are accomplished, it is not to judge followers' personalities. Keep this distinction in mind if you want to avoid interpersonal problems with your followers. The surprising truth about performance appraisal is that it is almost universally disliked by manager-leaders and followers. The process reeks with criticism, defensiveness and one-sided judgment. Animosities it creates may linger for years. True, manager-leaders who conduct performance appraisals are rarely trained properly, but the gut issue is that the process is all wrong. We have evaluated the person and not the performance.

Manager-leaders think they have learned much psychology. We know therapists can help people become better human beings, and in the name of goodness and justice, manager-leaders have tried to do the same. Manager-leaders are not therapists and should not attempt therapy. When asked to discuss employee counseling, I refuse. I tell manager-leaders not to counsel other human beings. However, we *can* talk about appraising performance toward objectives.

Manager-leaders have tried—in 45 minutes or so—to discuss everything about performance with a follower, and to make plans for improvement. Frequently, the appraisal is written and shown to the person. Dissenting opinions may be filed through proper channels. What competent therapist would sit with a client and tell everything—problems and plans for improvement—in one session? The skill of a therapist seems to be what not to say and when not to say it, rather than what to say.

The timing of appraisal has also been mishandled. Usually it is scheduled and periodic, rather than timely and continual. If I were to ask when you would prefer to examine your successes and failures, you would probably say, "at the time I succeed or fail." Most people want immediate feedback. When we talk continually, rather than periodically, we talk about performance rather than personalities, because the events are fresh in our memory. If we wait, details fade, and our only recourse is to talk about the person in front of us. We can still talk periodically, perhaps once a year, for an overview and some long-range planning, but not about specific successes or failures.

Many people believe criticism is a fundamental and necessary ingredient for improvement. The argument is that a person has a right to be told when his or her performance needs improvement. This right is not the issue. Criticism almost always becomes personal, a direct assault on a person's self-image.

The keynotes of modern performance appraisal are interaction and freedom of expression. The process now is a mutual examination by a manager-leader and follower of their performance toward objectives to determine how well they have cooperated and supported each other. It is an obvious extension of a participatory style of management and leadership.

Entirely new kinds of questions are being asked in the process. How well do you feel you have performed? How do you see yourself functioning in your areas of responsiblity? What are your expectations? What problems do you have about job knowledge, your ability to perform, getting along with others?

Appraisal forms are only guides, with plenty of white space, not "fill in the blank" or "mark the appropriate box." The forms are adjusted by each manager-leader to be meaningful in each situation and may be used in whole or in part as is most helpful. The form focuses on objectives—quantity of work, quality of work, resource scheduling, resource protection, cost control, education, laws and policies and communications as found in the follower's job description.

Some manager-leaders complete the appraisal and discuss it with the follower. Other manager-leaders ask the follower to make a self-appraisal first. The obvious third method is for both of them to develop their own appraisals and discuss them with each other. Do it the way it works best for you and your followers; adapt and relate. The important aspect is that the relationship is different. No finger of blame is pointed in either direction. Rather, both participants in the process of getting things done are working at how they can work effectively together.

Let's look at an example of interaction involving the objective of cost control when use of supplies is not being recorded by the follower. "It's difficult to keep track of all these things when you are in a hurry. You grab something and forget to mark it down." In a traditional system where we are hung up in personalities, a manager-leader could easily fall into a trap: "You're not careful enough about recording the supplies you use. You have to make a better effort to keep track of these things. Money is important." Criticism. Authoritarian admonition. Make people fit the system. We've heard it all before, and we'll continue to hear it unless we can find a new relationship. The manager-leader heard the content, but not the feelings, of human fallibility. The leader wasn't listening for the real problem.

Suppose the manager-leader said, "I wonder if there might be some simpler way of recording the use of these supplies?"

The follower might say, "Well, maybe if we had a form to fill out, or better yet, I wonder if somehow the items couldn't be tagged? What if we could just pull a tag off the item?"

"That would certainly be quicker. Let's see how we can approach this."

A new way of managing and leading? For many people, yes. How stubbornly we resist finding new and better solutions to our problems!

What you do depends on how much you want to manage and lead in a different manner. There is some flexibility in almost any system. Most personnel appraisal forms leave space for additional comments. Use it! Augment the system with your own ideas.

Disciplinary action warrants special attention. When we get to the rough practice of issuing written warnings and disciplinary suspensions, we're almost at the point of no return. Nevertheless, in the interest of salvaging a relationship, every effort must be made to work out misunderstandings. Discipline has traditionally been considered punitive, although in recent years we have tried to consider it corrective. Discipline by any other name, however, is still discipline. Perhaps the disciplinary procedure is best described as a method.

When do you discipline a follower? When the standards of normal and orderly behavior have been violated, and when you know why the standard was violated.

What is the disciplinary process? (1) Understand the situation. (2) Ask yourself, is discipline necessary? (3) Decide how much discipline is necessary to regain normal and orderly behavior. (4) Talk with the person.

What forms of discipline are available? Talk about the problem before you use the more formal and dramatic forms such as written warnings. Next, put your thoughts in writing. Sometimes this works, because it demonstrates that you aren't just talking. By writing I don't mean filling in a form that has a big, bold title saying "disciplinary warning." If you've devoted a substantial effort to the person and now feel forced to put your feelings into writing, I think you will want to say something more personal in the form of a letter:

1. stating the facts as you see them,
2. referring to previous discussions, and,
3. defining future conduct.

Sometimes talking and writing still does not get the message across. We're getting close to the end, but you should make one more effort, such as suspension. It is, of course, the most obvious way to demonstrate your intentions. Seek advice as you proceed, check out your own attitudes and actions.

The interaction between a manager-leader and follower will never be perfectly smooth; more realistically, at times it will become quite disagreeable. The measure of quality in the relationship is its success in resolving differences and working toward objectives together, not in a win-or-lose contest—blaming, finding fault, or judging—but with mutual support and understanding.

## How to be more effective

Most performance appraisal systems attempt to measure the personal traits of followers, or how well they behave. Instead, performance criteria should focus on desired results.

Using the job description example from chapter five—

*Helps customers and visitors by greeting them and referring them to the appropriate area.*

Here is a traditional "scoresheet" in behavioral terms used to measure job performance:

| | |
|---|---|
| **Distinguished:** | *Unusually friendly and helpful.* |
| **Excellent:** | *Usually successful in overcoming problems.* |
| **Average:** | *Approachable and likeable.* |
| **Below Expectations:** | *Keeps people at a distance.* |
| **Unsatisfactory:** | *Inconsistent and irritating in dealing with others.* |

Performance criteria are more effective when they are tied directly to a job description, use job language, and are written in a results-oriented format:

***Exemplary (what a follower does that is an example for others to follow)***
   *Start with a verb (or adverb)*
   *Do not state superlative (e.g., plans* better *than most people*
***Standard of Performance (the effect when the job is performed up to expectations)***
   *Start with a noun*
   *Write in the present tense*
***Improvement (what knowledge or skill typically must be acquired to attain the Standard of Performance)***
   *Start with "Needs to"*
   *Do not describe what a person should do "more" of or be "better" at, or what "knowledge of" or "understanding of" is needed*
***Problem (what happens if the Standard of Performance is not met)***
   *Start with a noun*
   *Do not state the opposite of the Standard of Performance*

Writing instruction examples:

| | |
|---|---|
| ***Exemplary:*** | *Remembers the names of customers and visitors who return; receives compliments of a helpful experience from customers and visitors* |
| ***Standard of Performance:*** | *Customers and visitors state that they feel good about their welcome, and arrive in the appropriate area without delay.* |
| ***Improvement:*** | *Needs to spend a few attentive moments with* |

|  |  |
|---|---|
|  | *each person; needs to learn building map and directory.* |
| **Problem:** | *Complaints of rudeness and disinterest are received; customers and visitors get lost in the building.* |

# Epilogue

# Will you change?

Other people may not agree with the changes you want to make in the way you manage and lead. You will have to determine the value of any change and its risk to you, and then decide whether you wish to continue. Changes involving human values are the most difficult.

Followers are rarely reluctant to participate in a relationship that touches their values. They welcome an opportunity to achieve goals that are important to them.

Your manager-leader, however, may hold different assumptions about the nature and behavior of people, or may not wish to have you take the time necessary to blend the goals of the organization with individual goals.

Success is not easy, but no one ever said it was. It is wise to start with small changes and build, instead of trying to make them all at once, but the important thing is to start, to take risks for what you believe.

What kind of person can be an effective manager-leader. Who can help followers find and use their motivation. Who has the spirit? I believe that a self-actualizing person would make a fine manager-leader: accepting of his or her own nature and of others, strong and disciplined, decisive, inventive, dignified and above the turmoil, unaffected by the obvious differences among people, and above all, spontaneous and natural without straining for effect.

Accept responsiblity for shaping your destiny. Pursue that destiny. Be aware of your impact and influence on others. Be open, not defensive or rigid to the reality that exists inside and outside of yourself.

This you can learn.